Praise for Sarah ...., MA

Homecoming is a return to the truth that inherently exists in each of us, a place where we can lovingly belong, nourish our soul and replenish our heart. Sarah has the gift of helping you find your Feminine (whatever that is for you) unapologetically, authentically, abundantly and audaciously - setting yourself free from the shackles of society and rise as the Queen you are. As you read each page, know Sarah is right there with you holding your hand and a safe space for you to shine. With every word she embodies the lost romance in everyday moments with a sense of abandon, where there's no space for shame - only a light and a knowing to the pathway HOME.

— Bindi Heit, podcaster and founder of the Ethical Change Agency

Whether you're a recovering Catholic, a witch still hiding in her broom closet, or a fully-out-there lightworker, this book is for you; it's for all of us. Sarah's words and her channeling of The Sacraments of The Goddess tenderly opened my heart up even more to receive the Love that was already there. A book birthed at just the perfect time as service to all women embodying this divine play on Mother Earth.

— Carleena Lara-Bregatta, author of *The Akashic Alchemist: A Cyclical Guide To Remembering Your Soul's Ancient Wisdom*

Homecoming is a gorgeously written work of HeART, dripping with truth-honey and feminine wisdom that deliciously invites you back HOME to your body, your being, and your Knowing. The Sacraments are Sacred Medicine that, when imbibed regularly, cultivate inner Wholeness and Holiness. Thank you, Sarah, for bringing this powerful and important work through and sharing it with us.

— Jaime Fleres, author of *Birth Your Story* and
Honoring the Whole

In reading this book, I was carried into the heart of the sacred Mother herself. It brings me great joy to surrender to the initiatory frequencies that leap from the pages into my feminine expression. I'm so grateful to receive and be in witness of Sarah's talent in connection to her own remembrance and creating a path of gold for others to walk upon for their own awakening.

— Marta Maria Marraccini, M.A., founder of
Quantum Belief, spiritualitywithmartamaria.co

I have witnessed Sarah Grady live her truth. In Homecoming, Sarah shares her journey with the reader in a voice that is equal parts bold, funny, raw and tender. If you are looking for a template to reclaim yourself, this may be the guide you've been seeking.

— Whitney Howard, Starland Alchemy

A raw, honest, touching exploration into what it means to come back home to the Source. Every chapter resonated as truth in my body, leaving goosebumps on my skin, tears in my eyes, and a reignited fire in my heart. This is a must-have guide to the Goddess-within for all modern day mystics.

— Jamie Kagianaris, filmmaker and founder of Period Love

Sarah Grady is like an old-style heroine, full of knowing sass and a deep desire to take way more than just a bite from the forbidden fruit of feminine wisdom. No wonder her words are flickering with the magic of Mary Magdalene. Enjoy the ride into the feminine queendom.

— Seren Bertrand, author of *Spirit Weaver*, coauthor of *Womb Awakening & Magdalene Mysteries*

I was captivated immediately. This book draws you in the same way Sarah herself does; calling you into deep presence with the Divine while encapsulating you with her radiant light. From this space she lays out a mystical yet practical approach to returning to the resilient and wise home within-a place of true sovereignty and belonging.

— Katie Veleta, Ph.D. Neuroscientist, science writer, yoga and AcroYoga Teacher

There are books you can't put down, and then there are books that won't let *you* down, long after you've finished reading them. This is one of those. It will grab hold of you in a place you didn't even know was in there, and transform you from the inside out. Required reading for every female-identified human, and highly recommended reading for everyone else, the sacraments outlined in this book are the homecoming guide so many of us have been searching for. Light a candle, grab your beverage of choice, find a cozy nook, and prepare to meet the Goddess within.

— Adrienne MacIain, Ph.D. best-selling author of
Release Your Masterpiece: A Powerful Guide to
Discover Your Authentic Gifts and Put Them to
Good Use

Homecoming

A Feminine GPS for a Lost World

Sarah Grady, MA

Red Thread Publishing LLC. 2022

Write to info@redthreadbooks.com if you are interested in publishing with Red Thread Publishing. Learn more about publications or foreign rights acquisitions of our catalog of books: www.redthreadbooks.com

Paperback ISBN: 978-1-955683-19-7

Ebook ISBN: 978-1-955683-21-0

To the women in my world:

This book is a prayer for all women. As such, I want to acknowledge the women who made it possible for me to even be here.

First and foremost, to the women of my lineage: to those who came before, the ones I never met in person, thank you for crossing oceans, surviving traumas, birthing babies, making beauty, navigating profound poverty and alcoholism, and still choosing joy and resiliency in the face of all of it. Because you survived, I am here. And because I'm here, may you now know a healing in your bones that wasn't possible when you were alive. May you know a rest, a rejuvenation and a freedom thought only to be a luxury for few. May you know that one of you now stands sovereign, at home in the Truth of who she is: sexually, creatively, and spiritually.

To the woman who birthed me, and the others who helped raise me: may you know that you don't have to work so hard anymore. May you know that your value isn't in the working, it's in the being, and that you're enough.You always have been.

*To the many I call sister-friends and soul family: thank you. Thank you for the midwifing and the mirroring. **We're doing it.** We're birthing the New Earth, one Sacrament, one voice memo, one hug, one* *leap of faith at a time. Thank you for fiercely standing in my corner, as I stand in yours. Thank you for standing for Love, for Consciousness, for Healing. Together, the impossible becomes possible every day. Keep dancing. I love you.*

A special thanks goes out to Laura Millichap, Kiala Givehand, Mary Julia Walker, Betsy Parker-Batista, my teachers Gabrielli LaChiara, Marta Maria Marraccini and Rochelle Schieck, the 13 original initiates of Homecoming, Red Thread Publishing, and of course, dearest Barry.

Contents

Opening Prayer

Beloved,

If you have found your way to this book, whether you know it or not, you are a woman connected to the sacred, the holy thread that weaves all of us back to the original Mother, source of all creation, the womb, of the womb, of the womb.

You are ready to lay down the armor around your heart. You are ready to let go of any structures, systems, beliefs or power dynamics that have kept you in line and captive as a "good girl."

You are ready to be vulnerable, to feel, to heal, to risk not knowing, or having the answer, or the next 10 steps of your life already planned out like a "smart" woman would.

You are a warrior of the heart who is tired of being tired.

Tired of pleasing, efforting, performing, and tap dancing for everyone around you while you lose yourself in the process. Tired of living status quo lives while you watch others take risks in the name of Love and Joy. Tired of toxic relationships, boring sex, traumatic sex, or no sex. Tired of your body being a burden instead of the absolute miracle that it is. Tired of overgiving and under-receiving, and tired of your bank account, your health, or orgasms reflecting that. Tired of being told you are too big, too emotional, or just plain too much. Tired of believing the myth that beauty is anything other than what you already are.

You are tired, but you are resilient, and you are *ready*. And you, dear woman, are a living, breathing, sacred, Sacrament.

By holding this book, you are signaling to the Universe and your own Soul that you are ready to reclaim your vital, precious, life force energy, and you understand that this reclaiming has powerful implications for yourself, your relationships, and the Earth. You are ready to reclaim your body as your own, your desires as sacred and not sinful, your mind as a brilliant servant to your heart, and your Soul, above all else, as your North Star of guidance on how you can show up in True service to yourself and the world. No martyrdom required.

In short, you are ready to come *home*. And my sister, it is never too late. If you have found your way to this book, you have already made a choice to choose your own aliveness, whether you know that consciously or not. You are ready to remember you have Choice. You are ready to birth yourself as sovereign, as worthy, as Queen of your own queendom. You are ready to reclaim the truth of your Divine Inheritance, which is this:

YOU ARE,

ALWAYS HAVE BEEN,

AND ALWAYS WILL BE

GOOD ENOUGH,

and not because you earned it, but because you exist, because you were born, and wrapped in skin, you are inherently GOOD ENOUGH.

Read that as many times over as you need to.

The truth is: **you are worthy**. And no one and nothing outside of yourself can ever give or take that away. It's cosmic law.

You, and only you, can know, align with, and practice the choosing of that Truth, and sister, it is a choice. So, this book is my prayer for all women to wake up to the choice of true Women's Liberation. Not the pantsuit-wearing, gotta slay in the sack AND be a boss-babe masculine bullshit we were sold in the 70's (which deeply overrides our own biological cyclical nature as creators of life) but true liberation from societal systems of oppression, which is what happens when a woman declares she is worthy of choice. Her liberation occurs when she authentically chooses from within herself and celebrates when other women do the same. A liberated woman does not compete or judge the free will choices of other women (or any gender for that matter).

My prayer is for women to choose to remember they have Choice. And in the rich, spiral journey of that heartbreakingly beautiful ride of grief and joy that it will surely be (because re-writing a 2000 year old history devoid of female choices ain't easy to do) I pray we slow down, take a deep breath, dust off our crowns, and reclaim what we have always known to be True: that you, yes you, and me, and all the women who came before, and all the women who will come after, are Queens. Not as some trendy concept, but as the embodied frequency of a woman who knows she is sovereign, walks through the world accordingly, and changes the world for the better as a result.

Under patriarchal systems women have been taught to outsource their own pleasure and power onto others (namely men, family systems, and government systems) as a way to keep women under control. Women who spoke their truth, connected to the Earth, explored their sacred sexuality, refused to marry or bear children they didn't want to, or express any emotion other than contentment, were deemed crazy, hysterical, witches, sluts, prostitutes, whores, insane, and the list goes on.

Women have been burned, tortured, enslaved, locked up in prisons or insane asylums, or held captive in suburban homes around America for daring to show up and speak up for a life worth living. The oppression of women knows no boundary of race, ethnicity, or socio-economic status. All women, whether sitting in board rooms or in unemployment lines have known what it is like to be treated as second class. Which is why this book is for every woman whose Soul finds a way to it.

The principles I speak of are simple and clear, but that doesn't mean they're easy. This is because of the world we currently live in. As I write these pages we are in a global pandemic. We are witnessing political and financial systems crumble before our eyes. We have never needed a roadmap to reclaim our sovereignty and our sanity so badly. This book was coming years before the pandemic, but the time for its proper birth is now, and in all the nows after this one. If we're honest, we can say that this collective crumbling, then awakening, reclaiming, and reorganizing has been long in the works. So here we are.

This book is an invitation, pandemic or no pandemic, to listen to the urgency of your own soul whispering "Sweet baby girl, stop, just stop, there's got to be a better way." And there is. There are many better ways. My book is just one offering in a sea of offerings that I hope you give yourself permission to explore as you re-member and reclaim who you really are.

You will notice that, throughout the book, I offer information on body-related topics such as herb lore,[1] womb work, etc. Please note that I am not a doctor, and this is not medical advice. Please consult with your inner wise-woman, as well as your team of trusted medical professionals, before trying any unprescribed product or embarking on any new course of treatment.

If this book inspires you to go deeper on your homecoming journey, I encourage you to join me for 1:1 mentorship, online courses, and international retreats where you can practice in real time with myself and other badass women on the path. To find out more about my offerings, and download your free Homecoming meditation, please head to www.sarah-grady.com

---

1. Many thanks to my herbal consultant, Mary Julia Walker.

How to Make the Most of This Journey

There is no right or wrong way to use this book or these Sacraments, though I do suggest reading about them the first time in order. This will fully initiate you at a cellular level to this blueprint. From there, by all means get creative!

Perhaps you use the Sacraments as a daily practice or mediation, a blueprint for your decision making process, a guide for your relationship life or financial life. Maybe you use them in order, or maybe there's just one that you lean on for guidance during a particular season in your life.

Trust that however you're being intuitively guided to use them is the best way for you. I can safely say that once you know them, all you have to do is say them aloud and their vibrational frequency will work with your higher self to guide you. If you never did an exercise in this workbook you would still get massive benefit from knowing these sacraments.

The Divine Feminine is non-linear, so let your journey with the Sacraments be a beautiful spiral path that leads you back home to yourself again and again in surprisingly authentic ways. This work is channeled to me and through me from the energetic frequency known as Mary Magdalene. Therefore, the nature of this work is both practical and spiritual; allow it to be both of those things for you.

This is to say: some days there will be practical, earthly actions you take inspired by the Sacraments to move your life forward. Other times these sacraments will be more of an energetic or metaphysical experience. Both, plus everything in between, is welcomed and encouraged. You always get to Sovereignly choose.

Honor Your Unique Lens

Many women from all walks of life experience Soul loss, and therefore a sense of spiritual homelessness. This is often because of acute and/or chronic trauma, which impacts a woman's nervous system, sense of safety, or even her sense of reality. There are also historical systems of oppression that deeply impact a woman's world view and sense of self. These systems often shape how women experience other women. As a white, cisgendered woman I cannot speak to how these Sacraments might serve the unique experience of women of color or women of the trans community.

What I can speak to is this: When one has become lost at sea, conscious and unconscious forms of cultural appropriation can ensue in an effort to find belonging, to find a sense of home again. My prayer is that this book offers a roadmap back home to oneself so that each woman, regardless of identity, may come to know, from the inside out, who *she* is unapologetically without needing to become someone else.

It can be scary and messy to go on the journey of learning who *you* really are, especially if you've always looked outside yourself for that answer. Especially if that answer was wrapped up in your safety and survival. But someday you'll wake up with a clear, unshakeable sense of self that will feel right in every way. There will be no need to people-please, fit in, or dampen desires. There will just be you, at home, in you, wherever you go.

Once a woman touches this internal sense of belonging, she can't untouch it. She may lose her way again from time to time, but the muscle memory of home will always call her back via the GPS of her body-temple and heart.

Trauma informed

Every single one of us has experienced trauma of some sort. To experience distress is part of the human experience. However, the impact of that trauma on your particular nervous system may look or feel very different than someone else who's experienced the same distress.

I cannot emphasize this enough: go slow. Based on past experiences, certain sacraments might feel confronting or nearly impossible. For instance, someone with a history of sexual assault or physical abuse might find it really hard to practice Sacrament 2...and that's OK. This work is not about pushing through or forcing an experience that doesn't feel right. It is 100% about reclaiming what does feel right and true to you, and no one else. Go slow and start small.

Each sacrament is simply an invitation. Perhaps some Sacraments will feel like second nature and others will take years or lifetimes to master.

There is no right or wrong, there is no one size fits all in the Feminine. There is only you honoring you.

Message to the masculine

If you are a man reading this book, bless you. If you are any gender reading this book, bless you. If you're in a body on the planet at this time, thank you for choosing to still be here.

It's my firm belief that you can benefit from these Sacraments, because all of us have been impacted by the construct of patriarchy. We've all been socially programmed to believe that being a "woman" or a "man" is supposed to look or feel a certain way. And yet, each of us carry an Inner Feminine and Inner Masculine energetically, regardless of gender.

May the practicing of the Sacraments flip society's script back onto your own personal script of who you BE and how you desire to relate to others and the Earth with love, respect, and care.

In interviewing several men during the writing process for this book, I came to understand that, at the core, both men and women are just looking for a greater sense of safety in themselves, their relationships, and in the world. We can't feel safe if our power is always being placed outside ourselves onto someone or something else. The sacraments bring you back home to yourself so you can get present to who *you* are, what *you* feel, what *you* know. Only from this presence or awareness can you begin to articulate your wants and needs to others.

Self-responsibility is a beautiful thing; the more we practice it, the less our relationships require defensiveness and the more every conversation becomes an invitation towards greater clarity. Clarity is grounding, clarity is sexy, clarity is inspiring, clarity is Love. And

Love doesn't have to have all the answers, Love doesn't have to have it all figured out, Love just is.

Permission, NOT perfection

The myth of patriarchy is rooted in perfectionism. If we can just look "perfect," or get the "perfect" scores in school, or have the "perfect" house, husband, and car, then we'll belong, then we'll feel safe, then we can finally take a breath and feel like we're allowed to be here on this planet.

The Divine Feminine understands that there's no such thing as perfect. She is wild, raw and real. She is spiraling and mysterious. She cares not for your preferred timeline, goal weight, or credit score. She cares about you being authentically YOU. Unless you're living in an indigenous culture, as a Western person, your cells are programmed at birth for perfection. The process of Homecoming is, instead, about permission. Permission to be you, to be messy, to fuck up, to feel, to express and embrace the totality of all of you.

As you go about the practice of each Sacrament, please remember that it is a practice. It is about giving yourself permission, not perfection. When a woman gives herself permission she gives all women around her that same permission, too. This is how we heal the wounds of history and begin to re-write herstory, from the inside out.

Outsourcing vs. insourcing

Each Sacrament is an invitation to support you moving from outsourcing to insourcing. This might feel awkward or uncomfortable at first, but take your time to read through each section and play with the workbook portion. Just a simple journal session with each sacrament can help you gain clarity and insight.

So, what do these concepts mean?

Outsourcing is the placing of one's power, pleasure, beliefs, values, desires, and knowing, onto someone or something else, including institutions, employers, and systems, in an effort to maintain safety and belonging (i.e asking what others think about something first before checking in with what you think or feel). Outsourcing often sounds like us "should-ing" on ourselves. When we are in the frequency of "should," it's usually because there is a tendril of guilt or fear present within us. We cannot be in love and fear at the same time.

Insourcing is the practice of creating space to turn inward to access one's own personal thoughts, beliefs, intuitive knowings, wants and needs (i.e. accessing what you think or feel about something first, and then engaging with others about it). When we insource first, it's a lot easier to come to agreements, compromises, and peaceful creative solutions with others because we are clear in our energy. Clarity is integrity. Other people respect integrity (unless they're raging narcissists). Outsourcing often puts us in the position of being taken advantage of because our center of control and personal power has been placed outside ourselves.

This is why, when we see someone totally frazzled and disembodied we say, "they're not home," or "they're clearly out to lunch," or "they're not operating with a full deck." Conversely, someone who is insourcing and connecting to self on a regular basis is HOME. In fact, they're often labeled as a "lightHOUSE" or beacon for others!

The biggest difference between the two is how you *feel*, and the Feminine is all about feeling. When we outsource our power and pleasure we often feel frazzled, drained, cloudy or stuck. When we insource, we often feel energized, inspired, alive and yet grounded.

Why now, why wait?

Systems and structures, as we've known them, are falling away; new ones are being built and ancient ones resurrected. There is no going back. To say that we are living in ungrounding times is a grave understatement. We can no longer place our sense of safety and belonging outside ourselves in social systems and institutions. We are being initiated, at a root level, to cultivate that sense of safety for ourselves internally.

My hope is that the process of *Homecoming* serves you to ride the waves of your personal life, and the larger waves of history, finding a sense of center no matter what is unfolding externally. Whatever "new normal" gets created will need to come from inside us if it is ever to be lasting and sustainable. No government, no magic pill is coming to save us. As the great Hopi elders prophesied in 2000, "We are the ones we have been waiting for."

In practicing the art of *Homecoming*, I hope every *body* comes to reclaim an audacious sense of joy, pleasure, and abundance radical to a capitalistic consciousness.

Joy in the face of crisis is the ultimate middle finger to a culture founded on our co-dependency and compliance. If we are the ones we've been waiting for, then why wait? It is time to choose your Sacred, Sensual, Sovereign life now. Your suffering and martyrdom are not required, they're not even welcome anymore.

Glossary

In modern-day Feminine spaces many of these terms get used. Below is a brief lexicon and how I conceptualize them as part of Homecoming. I encourage you to find your own definition, always.

Sacrament: per Merriam-Webster a sacrament is a Christian rite (such as baptism or the Eucharist) that is believed to have been ordained by Christ and that is held to be a means of divine grace or to be a sign or symbol of a spiritual reality.

*Sacrament re-defined: In the Sacraments of the Goddess, we understand that a Sacrament is not a holy rite that exists outside ourselves or ordained by someone outside ourselves. We re-member and re-claim that we are a Sacrament embodied. We are holy rites wrapped in skin. We ordain ourselves again and again every time we practice or embody the 7 Sacraments of the Goddess. We crown ourselves Queen, no one else is required.

Goddess: The omniscient and energetic presence of the Divine Feminine

Queen: The Goddess Embodied on Earth in human form

What constitutes a Queen is threefold:

1. Her choice to declare she is worthy of choice

2. Her capacity to exercise that rite daily as she goes out and lives the most audaciously sacred and mundane life she can, moment by moment, choice by choice.

3. Knowing when to walk away from people or situations that do not value and respect her as Queen, without apology.

Priestess: A Queen devoted to something she's passionate about, which could include a specific devotion to a Goddess or Deity, but can equally be applied to her love for her garden, an artform, or social cause.

Home: *Home* is not a place one arrives at, it is a feeling of profound resonance with oneself in relationship to another. Sometimes that "other" is a person, a parcel of Earth, a piece of music, or the smell of perfume. When a woman experiences a sense of home in herself and in the world, she can't un-experience it. She will forever know the imprint of what it feels like to belong in her own life, and she will no longer settle for things that feel less than.

As you embark on your journey home, I invite you to ponder what the word "home," means to you now. Then notice, without judgment, how your personal definition of it evolves throughout the book, one Sacrament at a time.

Introduction: Up in Flames

Sitting in a circle of women, eyes closed and heart open, *She* came to me.

Like a lightning bolt, wasting no time to deliver my next sacred assignment, the presence of Mary Magdalene appeared. She simply whispered, "I ask you to commit to being on fire with me for a year. If you do, you'll watch your whole life change."

I opened my eyes, and sitting across from me was my then-fiancée, whom I'd decided to leave just two weeks prior. My whole life was *already* changing. I had nothing to lose and everything to gain by saying YES.

I closed my eyes again and placed my hands on my heart. I asked to feel Her energy. She came closer. All in one flash, I felt Mary Magdalene as a Mother, Lover, Sister and Friend. The totality of what it means to be a woman. The current of what it means to be sovereign. The energetic embodiment of Love. I felt trust. I felt familiarity. I felt

Truth leading me, right there in that living room in the Oakland Hills.

She said it again, but this time with more assertion, as if she was about to walk me across a threshold, as if there was no going back. Because, of course, there wasn't. "I ask you to commit to being on fire with me for a year, and watch your whole life change."

Full-bodied chills and simultaneous wave after wave of heat moved through me. Yes. Just YES. A sacred, holy HELL YES. It emerged from so deep within me. There was no going back, and I didn't want there to be. I was ready for the more of me.

See, it wasn't that my life had been totally wrong, but it also wasn't totally right. And as far as I could tell, if what I wanted was a life that felt right in every way, I had to burn this one down and start over, from the ground up. From root to crown. Start from something more honest, and find my way home again, as terrifying as that might be.

I wrote my commitment to Mary Magdalene in my journal that night. I had no idea what it meant or where it would take me, but I had the readiness of a toddler, determined to take her first steps. I trusted that Magdalene, the loving Mother, would be there to guide and witness my crossing into the next stage of freedom, so I would never have to plan an escape route from my life again. I trusted the spiritual muscles in me that had been training for years to co-create with the Divine. Every healing session, every workshop, and every circle (of which there are many when you live in California), were all preparing me to walk home.

As someone who identifies as a psychic intuitive, or channel, I can say that my experience with Mary Magdalene that night was different from any other channeled experience. This wasn't me stepping aside to retrieve guidance for someone else's healing journey. This was me, fully present in my body, more than I had ever been, receiving what I had so deeply given to others throughout the years: hope. A ray of hope that if I answered the call of my Soul to burn the house down, in its wake I would find home. And most importantly, that I wouldn't be alone on the journey.

She came to me that night because, in deciding to leave my fiancée, what I had really done was call out to *Her*. Her visitation was proof that someone was listening.

May *you* always know that someone is listening.

There is nothing that could make you unworthy of this support. Your healing and your homecoming will not happen in a vacuum, I guarantee it. But first, the burn. In the fire of letting go may you find the courage and strength to let in all the goodness you didn't think possible before.

In the flames that followed in the year ahead I transformed from a Bay Area vegetarian, lesbian, psychotherapist to an East Coast doula who ate meat in *all* the ways, if you catch my drift. Perhaps your journey back home won't be so extreme, but I trust that it will be equally as honest.

And isn't that what we all crave anyways? A life beyond social media likes and promotions up the corporate ladder. But instead, a life built upon the sweet sweat of something real.

If you call for Her, She will come. If you yearn for that life, the steps will be shown.

Origin Stories:

To put it mildly, I was burnt the fuck OUT! I'd recently quit my job as a psychotherapist in community mental health. I was attempting to launch a private practice, blending my foundation in counseling with more shamanic energy healing work. I was living in the Bay Area, so that undoubtedly meant I needed 3 jobs in order to pay for life while waiting for my practice to take off. I'm pretty sure I traded one version of burnout for the other, but hey, at least it was the one that felt more authentic to me.

I nannied for a wealthy family in Oakland. You know, the kind that got flown in on a helicopter to Burning Man (true story!). I waited tables at a local restaurant that often called me off the day of my shift (that was cute for my ever-dwindling bank account). And, by the grace of the Goddess, I acted as rental coordinator for Terra's Temple, the then modern-day priestess temple in the heart of Berkeley, California. You know, like ya do. It was the job I loved the most and was of course paid the least for. But neither this book, nor anything that happened since my days at the temple, would've been made manifest if it wasn't for my time there. So, I am forever grateful for the plot twist life handed me with $15/hr and a global circle of change-makers that helped me rise to my destiny.

As the rental coordinator for the temple, I met with everyone who was considering renting the space. In other words, I had the blessing of meeting with healers and artists from all over the world to ensure the space fit their needs, and that their work was in alignment with our values.

Although there were some weirdos along the way, I was mostly astounded by the caliber of people who I crossed paths with, some of whom are my dearest friends to this day. Each of these healers reflected something back to me about myself, they seemed to say: dare to be bigger, dare to be who you really are, Sarah. Don't hide behind the safe or powerful label of therapist. Allow yourself to be the full embodiment of who you came here to be. Week in, week out, I met with people who seemed to reflect back that it was possible to do one's sacred work in the world without compartmentalizing that work into digestible pieces for different crowds or governing bodies. That instead, it was possible to weave together a synergy of one's gifts and talents into one body of work, one holistic expression. And this was important to me, because I'd already seen where the system of therapy was failing people of all ages. That we all needed a more holistic approach, not just to therapy but to all of life, if we were ever going to truly heal, evolve, or change. And that most of all, our bodies and the Earth Herself were depending on us making this change, and swiftly!

To have received this divine wink from various renters to keep pursuing my unique path would've been enough, but the Universe had something else up its sleeve.

Now, it's important to note that as I was struggling as a burned-out therapist, I was taking responsibility to do my own personal healing work with a counselor and spiritual guide. In one of our sessions together, my counselor channeled the message that I would one day create my own body of work; that my training and work as a therapist was not in vain, but that it was in service to whatever this ultimate body of work would be. I carried that knowledge with me for years until the Universe collided me with the reason for that message in Terra's Temple.

Along came Barry

One of my favorite renters at the temple was a Jewish elder. I love "old" people. I've been blessed to have incredible relationships with my grandparents in this lifetime, and I genuinely love listening to elders tell stories or reflect on their experience.

In fact, as a child, I always had friends who were older than me, always seemed to fit in with the older crowd-often preferring to be alone in nature with my crystal collection (not much has changed) instead of socializing with peers, because I felt I had to dumb myself down to do so. I was always so much more at home sitting across a table from my granny sipping tea than out on the playground talking about Beanie Babies and cartoons.

So, when Barry came to the temple to talk about the space and his renting needs for the Jewish elders circle he was running, I was ALL IN. Whenever he'd come by, I'd pull up a chair and just listen. I was fascinated by his faith, his sense of community and belonging, his connection to ritual and spirituality outside of dogmatic religion, and I was honored that he would share his time and heart space with me, a young 30-something non-jew.

After a couple years working for the temple, I received the divine nudge to close my life in California and begin a new chapter on the East Coast, returning to my home state of North Carolina. More to this story soon, but for now, it's important to know that after emailing my renters to let them know of my transition, it was Barry only who asked if he could come to the temple and bless me up before I formally transitioned out. I was so touched and honored, and immediately invited him to come by the temple anytime!

The day came for our sacred meeting. Barry, who, by the way, had the kindest eyes and the roundest belly that just made me want to squeeze him, entered the temple and per usual I gathered chairs for us to sit in and get cozy. Usually, we'd sit down and Barry would begin to recount a story or speak about his desire to support his community. This time, however, he leaned right in and said, "Sister Sarah (which immediately made me feel like I was a nun), you've been so kind and generous with your time, always listening to me when I come to the temple. But today, I want to listen to you. I want to know your story. How did you come to your faith? How did you get to be a woman working at a modern-day priestess temple, a sacred space in devotion to Terra, the Earth Mother, the Divine Feminine? Please, share. I want to know." I was floored. He wanted to know about *me*?!

Before I began to tell him my story, I felt everything in the room shift. My body, trained for subtle shifts in energy from a young age, knew something important was about to unfold. I felt my spine straighten, my crown lift, my heart open, and I felt the need to go slow so I could choose my words wisely-this wasn't a flippant exchange, this was a sacred one.

Origin Story of Sarah

And so I began my story, just as I began my life, as the product of an Irish-Catholic mother and an atheist father, who divorced when I was young. I told Barry how, even though my mother was extremely conflicted about the Catholic church, and its grave misogyny, it was all she knew. She wanted me to be connected to God, and having grown up going to Catholic school, my mom did find beauty in the ritual of the religion. My dad thought it was all (and by all, I mean every organized religion under the sun) royally fucked up and filled with hypocrisy. Out of these two extremes, the Catholic side won, and I and their progeny got shuffled around in a joint custody arrangement of mixed messages (both in day-to-day life, and in the Godly life.)

In other words, my family almost never went to church, except the obligatory Easter Sunday, occasional Christmas, or a funeral. And yet, my mom felt strongly that I was to receive my Catholic *Sacraments*. My parents shared joint custody of my brother and I, so every Friday I'd switch homes, and opposing ideologies, on just what the fuck this whole "life" thing was really about.

Before I dive into what the Sacraments are and how they continue to weave in and out of my life, I think it's important we get something straight right off the bat. I use the word FUCK a lot. Despite my parents being diametrically opposed in most areas of life, what they both can agree on is the emphatic language of being Irish-American, raised in New Jersey. Fuck is fire, but to me, and my family, it's a holy fire. Truly a sacred word. If this doesn't resonate, well, it just doesn't, but I do hope you'll hang in there to read about the Sacraments anyways. They truly are life-changing, no cursing required.

Both my parents come from this Irish lineage, both come from FIRE. Both parents are adult children of alcoholics. Each dealt with that trauma very differently. Fire is a tricky element when you're Irish. We're a fiery bunch, known for our hot tempers and brooding moods, but if kindled correctly, the fire is the most potent alchemical element of inspiration and creativity.

My ancestors liked to drink. A lot. But they also liked to tell stories. I grew up around a deftness of words that would put most people to shame. Wit, charm, cunning poetry of conversation and debate. The oracular tradition is strong, though in my experience, not particularly honest. What do people who hold so much brilliant fire inside do when they don't live in a world that knows how to help them hone that fire authentically? Or frankly, if they're just too poor to access support? They drink or they repress, or both.

"Don't tell the business" was one of my granny's famous lines. Funny thing though, "the biz" always has a way of getting out. And for me, and my business, which was a deep knowing, even pre-verbally as a child, that we were all connected to something so much larger than all of us, that God had nothing to do with church, and that my body was sacred and holy, that biz, it turns out, would eventually become my life's work.

Although this work didn't formally begin until I was in my 30's, the seed of it began as a young child. I remember reading books about ancient Egypt and Native Americans, especially the Hopi tribe of the Southwest, and feeling a visceral connection that seemed to make way more sense in my body than that of the Catholic church. I asked my dad to take me to a Native American pow-pow being held at our town's civic center when I was in elementary school. I'll never forget the sensation of aliveness and Truth I felt when we approached the ceremonial tent. Even as a child I cared not for souvenirs: I wanted to touch God the way the dancers' feet kissed the dirt of the Earth that day, the way the drums beat, the way the voices carried ancestral messages through their chant and song. I wanted to be that alive, that connected, that loved by Creation and my community the way these Native people were.

The only times I came close to that sensation outside that environment was when I was dancing or swimming. Childhood fascinations included dolphins, whales and the Little Mermaid, for little did I know the archetypal medicine each offered, and what I'd later learn to be beings deeply connected to "God" through various star systems and ancient civilizations. And dancing, oh, my first and only ever true love. My mom, to her credit, put my first pair of ballet slippers on my feet at age 3 and I never looked back. I hated wearing real clothes, but would parade around the house in bathing suits and leotards proclaiming "mommy, I'm a dancer" with Paula Abdul and Janet Jackson on full blast. I am a child of the 80's afterall. Everything in the world melted away when I danced. When the music came on it was just me and God. I still feel this way, whether dancing by myself, facilitating a class, or attending a performance. But dancing would later prove to speak to something larger, which I cover in Sacrament 2 of this book: **embodiment**.

To be present in the body, to go deep into our hearts and our sensual experience, this is the direct conduit to God, in my experience. And this is in both direct harmony with the ancient teachings of the Divine Feminine and simultaneously direct conflict with modern day Christianity. To be in the body, especially in a state of pleasure, is considered sinful in the Catholic church. So, at age 3 with my ballet slippers on, I might as well have started shouting to all who would listen, "Mommy, I'm a sinner. A really big sinner. I love sinning. I love it so much I'm going to devote my whole life to it!" A bit dramatic, I know, but hey, I literally have two degrees in theatre. Let's not talk about how early I started masturbating and all the past life memories of sacred sexual temple priestesshood I would come to re-member again, and again, and again.

In addition to dance, I remember buying my first book on yoga at age 12. I just had the sense that I needed to learn as many ways of being in my body as a sacred act as I could. That same year, I also asked my dad for Buddha statues I found in a Barnes & Nobles for (Christ)mas. Even in suburban North Carolina, where there were more churches than grocery stores, there was still hope inside a chain bookstore for my little sacred rebel heart!

In middle school, one of my best friends was East Indian. I remember she returned from a family trip to India one summer and brought me back my first Ganesha statue. A beautiful soapstone figurine of the elephant-headed Hindu deity known for removing obstacles. I still have this statue sitting on my altar at home. All that it unlocked for me around spirituality being playful, colorful, fun, and feminine were invaluable lessons at the time. In high school and college I read everything I could get my hands on about other cultures and religions, not to fetishize them, but to hopefully put language to the thing I felt inside. I was on a constant quest that followed me through my many life chapters in Boston, Los Angeles, Chilean Patagonia, and the San Francisco Bay Area where dear old Barry and I intersected.

Often my spiritual journey deepened with experiences of loss, grief or trauma-nothing like an abusive boyfriend or the pain of an eating disorder to wake me up to Love. Time and time again, God was there, saving my ass from myself and all that my sweet soul chose to initiate me into. More and more, I could see evidence in my life that God wasn't a punishing force outside myself, but a deeply Loving force that wanted to co-create with me from within me.

And more often than not, God was she, a Goddess. She came to me as Bridgit from Ireland, Isis from Egypt, Quan Yin from China, Kali from India, Yemaya from Africa, or Aphrodite or Athena from the Greek pantheon. She was strong and fierce, but also deeply sensual, sexual, alchemical and loving. She was multi-faceted, and She reflected the multi-faceted, multidimensional nature of human women. She had grief and pain, she experienced lust and desire, she felt rage and terror, and she was also the embodiment of peace. All of which I, you, we experience and express as women on planet Earth. She wasn't bad or wrong, She was real. And she let me know every step of the way that I was real, and that it was ok to be really *me*.

So, what is a sacrament? A spiritual rite of passage that, once received, signals belonging in the church and the worthiness to receive grace. The 7 Sacraments of Catholicism are: Baptism, First

Holy Communion (Eucharist), Confirmation, Reconciliation, Anointing of the Sick, Marriage, and Ordination (Holy Orders).

My mom insisted on my Baptism, First Holy Communion and Confirmation. Reconciliation, or Confession, is something I could do with a priest anytime I went to church if I wanted. But like, really, what 10, 12, or 15 year old wants to tell an old celibate white dude, a.k.a. priest, that they've sinned? How the hell is he going to understand, and why does he have to be the intercessor for God? Why can't I just talk to God myself? Oh, and by the way, why is EVERYTHING I DO somehow wrong in the eyes of the church?

The very few times I did actually go inside a Catholic church as a child, all I ever felt was wrong. Like I was doing [it] wrong, like my body was wrong and needed to be controlled, like even my thoughts and heart's desires were inherently wrong or sinful.

I mean, way to win someone over: tell them how horribly wrong they are all the time! That's a winning strategy to create Love and Unity! (My cynical atheist father's voice is coming out—hey dad, you proud?!)

So, as soon as I got the hell out of North Carolina and started theatre school in Boston, I continued my quest for knowing my inherent goodness in the eyes of God. Ironic that Boston was the first place my soul would choose to do this kind of spiritual work, but I digress.

Back to Barry

I told Barry all of it. All the adventures from every city I ever lived in. All the beauty, all the trauma. All the ways in which I beat up my body and then learned to love it. All the love. All the loss. All the times I rose like the Phoenix, even when I had no idea how I'd pay the rent. And then I told him one more thing.

I said, "Barry, for all the times I felt forced into Catholicism or felt enraged by the narrative of God being a big white man in the sky outside myself watching every 'wrong' move I was making, despite how hard I tried to be a 'good' little girl, there was one moment connected to this religion that felt different, markedly different."

He grinned ear-to-ear and leaned in for a deeper listen.

"Barry, my granny, to whom I'm deeply connected, who is with me in spirit every day, she and I used to pray together. When she and my grandfather retired, they left New Jersey and moved to South Carolina. I'd go visit them every Summer, and one of the most special memories I have is laying in bed with her, especially during big Southern rainstorms, praying the rosary. My granny always had a lavish canopy bed, and a room filled with beauty. Just getting to cuddle her every night was a treat. She kept the tradition of praying the rosary every night before going to sleep. Once I received my First Holy Communion, at age 7, my granny knew that I now knew how to say the Hail Mary prayer of the rosary. There wasn't much else I enjoyed about the process of receiving my First Holy Communion, but there was always something soothing about reciting that prayer. Perhaps, because it was one of the few things oriented towards the feminine. In other words, every time I said that prayer, I felt myself as a young woman in the world being seen and acknowledged, and representation matters. So, when the rains would start to pour, and the sky pitch black filled with Southern scents of mint and magnolia from the garden, my granny and I would pull out the rosary beads and pray. It felt like we were in our own little world. It felt like we were outside of time and space. All wrongs were being righted. It felt like we were part of a secret society of women; a society where we all knew I was good, and that the world was good, too.

"We prayed to Mary, but we mostly prayed *with* Her. I didn't feel any of the weird power dynamics I felt in church. I just felt a loving presence. That love would beam through my grandmother's eyes or in the carrier wave of her voice, or in the softness of touch when she'd play with my hair or rub my cheeks as we prayed. And even if I didn't have words for it at the time, I also felt the presence of Mary, of The Mother, and I knew it to be as real as the touch of my granny's fingertips. It was the same presence I felt when I was dancing, or swimming, or talking to Nature."

I paused, with tears in my eyes and decided to take a breath. I wasn't sure if I had bored, overwhelmed, stunned or intrigued Barry with my entire life story. But the next moment would prove to be one of deep understanding, or innerstanding, should I say.

Just as swiftly as I took one breath of pause, Barry placed one hand on my shoulder, as if anointing me with a sword, and said, "Well then, sister Sarah (the irony not lost on me), my prayer for you, as you leave California and return to North Carolina after all these years, is this: may you allow yourself to fully release the Sacraments of Catholicism, and all that did not serve your connection to God in that religion. And may you come to know, learn, embody and teach THE SACRAMENTS OF THE GODDESS."

And there it was, like a fucking lightening bolt up my spine! A direct message from God Herself. Everything in that moment stood still. I knew Barry was merely the conduit for The Mother of all of creation.

In that moment, I received my sacred assignment. I received it because I needed it. But I had a suspicion that all women everywhere needed it. For every woman who was tired of being told to be good for a system that never wanted to actually acknowledge her goodness. For every woman who never fit into the systems she tried so hard to be good for, religious or otherwise. And for the Earth Herself, who was aching for us to remember our goodness so we would stop destroying Hers in an attempt to assuage our grief. This was my assignment. I didn't know what it was in form, but I knew I was ready to listen and to show up in service to it for the rest of my life.

Barry and I didn't say much after that moment. We embraced for a long hug and he thanked me for all I did in my role at the temple. I waved him goodbye and I thanked his Soul, deeply, for changing my life that day.

(Insert joke about what happens when an Old Jewish man and a recovering Catholic Millennial walk into a priestess temple LOL!)

Coming into Form

A month later, I packed up my belongings and drove cross-country from California to Carolina.

Although I grew up in NC, I'd never really spent much time in the mountains, so it was an interesting sacred call when my Soul told me to move to Asheville, NC. The Appalachian mountains are debatably the oldest in the world. They know things. And when they call, they pull you in like a fucking tractor beam of light. There's really no choice in the matter. I arrived ready to heal my body and heart from the hustle of nearly 10 years on the West Coast. I arrived, attempting to make sense of the complete 180 my life had taken, and deeply curious about these Sacraments of the Goddess.

About a month into my new life in Appalachia, a region which, coincidentally, many Scots-Irish people settled in post-famine, I decided to sit down at my altar and open myself up to the sacraments. I called in my ancestors and the ancestors of the land. I called-in my guardian angels and frankly any other beings of light that were there to support this process. I lit a candle, anointed my body with some oil, and I prayed, "Okay, whoever you are, whatever you are: I am open. I am humble. I am here. I am ready to receive the Sacraments of the Goddess."

And almost immediately, just as She had come during summer rainstorm rosary sessions with my granny, Mother Mary appeared.

By appeared, I mean the presence of Her energetically arrived. I felt Her at the back of my heart, as if to create some sense of reassurance or comfort. Then the presence of Mary Magdalene appeared, this time at the front of my heart. I'd been working with the presence of the Magdalene for months leading up to this moment, so I was familiar with Her energy signature. She felt like a dear old friend: earthy, sensual, strong, and deeply loving in her presence.

Almost immediately, Mary Magdalene said, "Okay dear Sarah, I will give you these Sacraments. They are really quite simple. But, they're not easy. This is because of the world you live in. This is also precisely why they are needed. The time for sharing them with the world at large will come. However, for now, write them down, shift the language as it makes sense to you, and then go out and live them. Do not teach them, or shout them from the mountain top. Live them. Let them live in you, and change your life. True teaching is about EMBODIMENT. So embody these sacraments to the best of your ability, and we'll let you know when it's time to reveal them."

And just like that, almost as swiftly as they appeared, Mother Mary and Mary Magdalene left. I blew out my candle. I stared at my journal in disbelief.

Then, I got to work.

I allowed my already-dismantled life to crumble, clarify, burn, and refine even further, so that I could be as naked as possible before Love. So I could actually allow the new life I'd been praying on my hands and knees for to arrive. Or shall I say, reveal itself to me, because once revealed we always, and I mean *always*, have free will to accept it or not. The choice is always ours.

Choice is the name of the game when it comes to Queendom; sacred, sensual, sovereignty. *You* are always in the driver seat, not some big scary dude in the sky. The Divine is merely there to guide you along the way.

Now, this isn't to say that all organized religion creates shame spirals of self-hatred. To the contrary, organized religion can bring a lot of hope and joy and beauty to people's lives. I've witnessed it first hand. Like anything, religion isn't black or white. And for those of us who have a propensity for learning how to hold the paradox of life, the 7 Sacraments of the Goddess offer us a pathway not just to radical self-commitment, but to radical compassion, for all of life.

This book isn't to say that I'm right and they're wrong. It's about honoring that it's *all* welcome, it's all valid, it's all perfect if it's in service to Love or Unity instead of separation or duality consciousness.

These sacraments came to me because I was way too young to be burned-out, losing my hair, breasts full of lumps, hands up to the sky wondering if I'd ever know Love, for self or from someone else! They came because I desperately needed a new way of approaching life, which says a lot considering I was already the empath black-sheep theatre major / woo-woo lesbian drama therapist family member, living in San Francisco and consorting with the divine feminine, NOT the jacked-up on caffeine and cocaine broker climbing corporate ladders or sailing the shark-laden seas of wall street. Imagine how those poor mother fuckers feel?! Shit!

If *I* was losing my shit, and I had all the tools in the world to regulate my nervous system or make seemingly empowered decisions other people did not, then Houston, we have a MAJOR FUCKING PROBLEM.

It's Time Now:

After receiving the Sacraments of the Goddess in Asheville, I ended up moving back to my hometown of Raleigh-Durham. Talk about the Hero(ine's) journey coming full circle!

I felt strongly that I needed a sacred vocation to pay the bills while I continued to live and process the sacraments. The word doula had been haunting me for years. I'd even declared on my psychotherapy website that I was a "dance doula," teaching weekly Qoya dance classes in addition to building my healing practice. Long story short, my year in Asheville was basically my year of training in all the things I'd put on hold during grad school, which included yoga teacher training and both birth and postpartum doula training. I came to the Triangle area and promptly began life as a full-fledged doula. Most of the work came in the form of postpartum care (I'll get on my soapbox about how the American birth system sucks later) but for now, all that matters is that I was busy!

For the first time in a long time, I had ONE job, not ten, doing something that not only paid the bills, but that I loved, and felt was sacred service. The Sacraments, however, kinda took a back burner.

I was enjoying a "normal" life for a hot minute. You know, the kind where you can afford groceries, and to actually buy people Christmas presents without putting them on your credit card. Well, it was nice while it lasted, because then Covid-19 hit. It derailed many plans for many people, myself included, but for me personally, it also created a massive opportunity.

The opportunity goes a little something like this:

Stay small and safe?

OR

Be brave, get bigger, shine your light, let yourself be seen for who you truly are, and BE and what you truly came here to this planet in service of. Which has a lot more to do with *being* than doing, let me tell ya.

So, my Soul, along with the sassy nudge of one of my favorite clients (and my only client during the initial stages of Covid), stepped forward to say YES. Yes to the thing that my entire 35yrs on the planet had been preparing for. Which was **not** to be the actress, teacher, therapist or even doula that I trained to be, but to stop hiding behind labels and rise as the vessel for the 7 SACRAMENTS OF THE GODDESS.

You know, the thing that will totally make sense to everyone when you tell them what you do for a living. *Not.*

This sacred call initially started with my dream to open a women's liberation center, called Queen. Although this dream became a "dream deferred" with the onset of the pandemic, with the savvy support of said sassy client, my dear friend turned business coach, and the love of many dear sister-friends around the world, I decided to pivot my physical center into this book, and into an online women's liberation center full of sacred classes to explore these sacraments virtually until we can gather again in person.

Y'all, learn the art of the pivot. It will teach you things about yourself you never knew were possible, and it will align you with your internal feminine essence faster than any crystal, oracle deck or fancy orgasm essential oil ever could. The feminine essence is wild, creative, and nonlinear. When we follow Her lead, employing more masculine actions along the way, such as filling out documents, making decisions, or creating structures/systems of support, damn, anything is possible!

And so it is. The woman who was burnt out and tossing the towel in on her own life is now showing up in service because of seeing that experience reflected in society at large.

Covid has placed a giant microscope on all of our systems, structures, beliefs, patterns of behavior, and societal norms, and is asking us to get very clear about what is actually serving us and what is NOT. Our bodies, relationships and Earth are breaking down because we've kept a patriarchal industrial pace that is harmful to our body's, relationship's, and Earth's natural rhythms and cycles.

We need to learn how to rest when it's time to rest, not to chug a Red Bull and push through. We need to learn when to let go when it's time to let go, so we're not codependently and desperately hanging on to relationships that don't serve our health. And we need to learn to respect the resources of the planet we're living on, or our forests will continue to burn as the ozone continues to burn, UV rays continue to burn our skin, and astronomical increases of cancers infiltrate our embodied "norm," for which there will surely be yet another pharmaceutical "solution" that will inevitably introduce a whole new set of problems.

In short, THE TIME IS NOW. And truthfully, the time is always now. When considering living a life that honors and respects the earth of your body and the earth of our planet, there's never a more "right" time than now. Zoom fatigue and all.

As Mary Magdalene told me, these Sacraments are simple, they're not easy. Still, I assure you, they are possible and they are a choice. No one is going to come celebrate you or berate you if you don't choose them. The measure will be in how you FEEL about your life and the world around as a result of engaging with them. These sacraments aren't given to you by a priest, or even a priestess. They are given to you, by you, and for you. This is the path of sovereignty. It's not dogma. It's just an offering in the sea of infinite offerings to getting to the same place we all want to arrive at in each now moment: LOVE AND BELONGING.

Mary Magdalene:

I want to be very clear, this book is not about Mary Magdalene. There are some amazing resources out there if you'd like to research Her further. Although, truth be told, there's not much "information" you'll find. For most, myself included, she is best known through personal experience, or that which we would call *gnosis,* in theological terms. Meaning, a direct experience of the divine (i.e. no intermediaries such as priests or pastors need to be present, it's just you and God/Goddess/Source/Creator/Whomever you pray to or commune with, having a conversation or energetic exchange in the moment). This is real *intimacy,* folks.

For me, I "know" Mary Magdalene like I know a good friend, She comes to me, directly. I feel her energetic signature, I hear the cadence of her voice, I feel her presence in my body. Just as Christians speak about having a relationship with Jesus Christ, I have a relationship with Mary Magdalene. She's the bomb, my home girl, home slice, BFF, sister-friend, mentor, mother, and guide all in one. I feel her and know her in this way because I am her. Audacious to say, but it's true. For those of us who feel the call, we're all waking up to the remembrance of ourselves as Her on the planet at this time. Because, after 2000 years of persecution and "all that carrying on," as my Nana used to say, it's time to return to Love.

You might recognize yourself as a Magdalene in your propensity for wearing the color red or green, like the robes she would wear when healing or teaching. It might be your affinity for essential oils or herbs, and the sacred acts of anointing the body with these tools for which She was so famously known, with her alabaster jar. Or perhaps it is your profound knowing that your body is holy, that sex is sacred, and joining your body with another in union is an act of the divine, *not* of sin.

Maybe you're inexplicably drawn to travel or move to Egypt, France, the British Isles or earth grids where healing is needed. Many of us will receive sacred assignments to move throughout our lives. This is not just a random desire.

Magdalene, for me, is an energetic presence that feels earthy, grounded, sensual, clear, mature, wise, honest, discerning, sexy, but most of all, deeply, deeply heart-centered. She's here, on the ground level with me, guiding my body through sensations of warmth, expansion, softness, tingles, or chills. She always leads me to people, places, and experiences that foster a greater sense of aliveness and love. She engages my 5 senses unapologetically. She returns me to my erotic innocence. She reminds me that every word I speak is sacred service. She's got my back and whispers to me in my womb.

Mother Mary feels light and graceful in her presence, while Magdalene keeps it real. We need both. Ya feel me?!

We need all emanations of the Divine Feminine, for human women are multifaceted, multidimensional beings, so why wouldn't the divine in feminine form be the same?

In other words, Mary Magdalene is my giant permission slip to take up space, spread my full wingspan and be fully ME. She does this because She is me, I am her, and we are one. She reminds me of this all the time. She's my higher self, if you will. And maybe she's yours too?

Here's the thing with the divine: when you're ready, it'll start to speak to you in all sorts of mysterious, beautiful, and sometimes hilarious ways. It'll be like someone obnoxiously knocking on your door until you answer. And when you do, get ready to come home.

Mary Magdalene helped midwife all that was standing in the way of me truly taking up residence in my own body and being, and when I was empty enough, She graciously gifted me the 7 Sacraments of the Goddess. No telling what She, or any other fractal of the Divine, will gift you! And P.S. it's all a gift. Even the hard, shadowy shit. In fact, those bits are usually the best gifts. Don't you know how a diamond is formed?

<u>From Mary Magdalene to You:</u>

Beloved,

You don't have to believe in me for me to believe in You.

And I want you to know how much I believe in you.

I believe in your inherent goodness, because you were born.

I believe your body to be a sacred, holy grail for that goodness,

For Love embodied.

I believe your pleasure and deepest desires to be holy indicators

of your Soul's blueprint

for sacred service in this life.

I believe your joy matters

I believe your experience of Love

is what literally heals the molecules

in every room you walk into.

I believe in your intelligence,

not the kind they trained you for at school,

But the kind that lives deep in the marrow of your bones,

The ancient parts of you that carry the ancient memory of me,

Of the holy temples all priestesses,

or Queens as you say,

were both employed in and revered for their embodied devotion to love.

I believe how tired you are,

and how you feel like there is no other choice but to keep enduring the current matrix of life

But I believe more in your capacity to break free from the cage of that matrix

so you no longer have to live a life of endurance

but

A life of truly

Living.

In

LOVE.

I believe that all your "crazy" ideas and notions, or wild emotions are really just your higher self, waving a white flag, saying:

"Pay attention! I am not a peasant, I am a Queen, and something in my life is out of alignment with that Queendom

and my body & being are letting me know in no uncertain terms that I can do something about it!"

I believe that you are stronger than you think, but that your greatest strength is your vulnerability

I believe that you are worthy of having a seat at the table with men

but you don't have to become one in order to keep that seat

I believe you are a wise, wild woman whom others look up to and into as TEACHER

For we are all teachers and

Mirrors.

There is no hierarchy,

only a circle of women and men

Around the world

rising and re-membering

LOVE

Together.

I believe you will stand for a life where your body's natural rhythms and cycles are honored,

Just as we are meant to honor the seasons and cycles of Earth.

I believe your heart compass knows the way

I believe in your belonging,

To self,

And to a circle of others (human, plant, animal or otherwise) that live to see you thrive

I believe you learning how to trust and love yourself is the greatest miracle of all.

I believe the mystery of life is always,

And I mean, always

Abundantly

Conspiring on your behalf.

And when it feels like it's not,

I believe in your resurrection,

Like a phoenix rising from the ashes,

Again, and again, and again

You

Rise.

I believe that rising in you

Is actually your ability to go deeper inside yourself

Every time you'd rather escape.

I believe in that deep place inside you

Inside me

That is the only Truth there is:

Love.

I believe you will always find your way back there

Because it is human nature to want to know

Where we come from.

We come from Love.

I believe in you.

Your Journey Home Starts Here

I'm rooting for you. The Sacraments are rooting for you. Love is rooting for you.

May your journey be blessed.

I'll meet you on the other side.

The 7 Sacraments of the Goddess:

Transmissions, Stories, and Practices

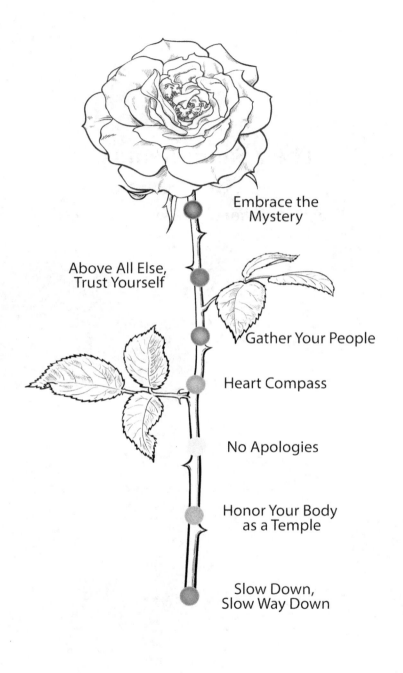

Embrace the
Mystery

Above All Else,
Trust Yourself

Gather Your People

Heart Compass

No Apologies

Honor Your Body
as a Temple

Slow Down,
Slow Way Down

Sacrament 1:

Slow Down, Slow Way Down

Re-membering

There was a time when we took time. When we paused long enough to take a breath, look each other in the eye, and listen.

There was a time when we extended this listening to the seasons and cycles of the Earth, a woman's body, our own Soul, and we had everything we needed.

There was a time when we were grateful for what we had, and didn't want more than what was before us. We were present to the bounty of every breath.

There was a time when our greatest technology was in our being, and not in our doing.

There was a time when life was slower. Easier. And it was easier because we were listening.

Remember this time.

Slow Down, Slow Way Down

"Nature does not hurry, yet everything is accomplished."

— Lao Tzu

Slowing down is the Sacrament of Sustainability.

Your life is not a sprint to get through, it's a spiraling journey and you deserve to have all the presence and energy for it possible. Declare your willing release of quick-fix paradigms here and now. Allow yourself to re-member a slower, more sustainable way of living and loving.

It may feel uncomfortable, it may bring up all sorts of guilt and shame because of how we have carved out an identity for ourselves based on how much we can produce and how quickly. Go slower anyway.

Allow yourself the process of becoming. You are just as worthy in the becoming phase as you are in your creation phase. If you need help remembering this, just watch a caterpillar morph into goo before it becomes a butterfly with wings.

When we embrace sustainability, it makes it a lot easier to live in the present moment with trust in the seasons and cycles of life and the feminine intelligence that moves things forward even when it appears they are standing still. We stop living for retirement or some distant finish line moment when everything will be less stressful and taxing on our system. Instead, we courageously embrace a better way. Not because facts and figures tell us it's better, but because we physically feel better in the process of it. Our sleep, our digestion, and our spirits all begin to sing in greater harmony.

When we're not rushing and pushing, we also tend to be kinder to ourselves and others. The slow, sustainable burn of enduring Love begins to guide our every move. You are worthy of the slow burn. You're worthy of a life you want to live, not just one you have to get through.

Make no mistake, the more sustainable life will require you to give up things your ego is deeply attached to. This is the process of homecoming. We let go of what doesn't truly serve us, so we can embrace what does.

In a world where your value is predicated on your productivity, the most radical thing you can do is slow down.

Disrupting the pattern

When we slow down, we disrupt the pattern of our current thought forms and behaviors. Disrupting the pattern of habitual thoughts and behaviors is key to making change.

Often this starts very small; taking a breath and saying aloud "slow down," in a moment where you would normally barrel through and react to the triggering email, answer the phone, or engage in an addictive habit. Over time, you begin to catch yourself in the body awareness of feeling frazzled or out of body, and recognize that you don't want to feel that way anymore. You then make small steps, like breaths or going for a walk, towards coming back into the body. Small steps, over time, that come from within you, create sustainable change.

Disrupting the pattern often supports us moving from reactivity to responsiveness. Slowing down helps create awareness on what programmed responses often occur in certain relationships or environments, and how we might try responding to those same things differently because we feel more grounded and centered in ourselves. Your reactive mode might be to always yell at your kids for not cleaning their rooms. Your responsive mode might look like creating a fun ritual or incentive for your kids to clean their room.

Instant gratification never tastes as good as the slow,
steady, acquired taste of alignment.

Ritual Activism and the Addiction of Busyness

I like to call Slowing Down "ritual activism." We live in such intense times, and it feels like at every turn there's a new wave of social and political upheaval calling us to action and activism. Not everyone is an effective activist standing on the frontlines of a protest. Sometimes it's writing a letter to Congress, sometimes it's deciding to no longer purchase foods with GMOs, and sometimes it's consciously choosing to rest and tend to your body in a world that profits off your dis-ease.

The addiction to busyness is real. And it makes sense: in a world where your value is predicated on your productivity, of course you want to stay busy because your busyness is deeply rooted in your belonging. Every time you decide to slow down when the world wants you to speed up, you are advocating for and activating an ancient belief resurrected: that your value is inherent to you being alive. Period.

Sister, you are not here to earn your keep. You are here to *be*. Your being is pure essence and energy, it is not something that can be quantified or commodified. That's why it's so terrifying to our current status quo. BE you anyway. The world needs you, all of you. All the beautiful, messy, brilliant, afraid and deeply desirous, loving parts. The emails can wait, your body cannot. We've all been there. If you don't slow down and listen to her, she'll find a way to force your slow down. Slowing down is the best preventative healthcare there is.

Slowing down creates space, so **it's important to create a space for the space**. When we slow down, we're effectively shutting out all the noise of the world, including other people's beliefs, energy, and opinions. In exchange, we create energetic space for us to hear, feel and access our own internal voice.

Homecoming

We can create space for ourselves anywhere we intend to. I've had many a "slowing down" moment on city subways and in crowded airports simply by turning on my favorite song and intending that I tune out outside input, close my eyes, and go inward. That being said, in my experience, it's easier to practice and integrate this sacrament by creating a physical space for slowing down.

I am a total proponent of every woman having her own sacred room. This could be a special room in her house, an outside shed, or an office space. A full room might not be possible, so in its place, I suggest a corner of a room. Find one corner of one room you can get to regularly, preferably daily, and create a physical structure that feels grounding and sacred.

I've been building altars on my bedroom dresser since I was a little girl without knowing that many indigenous cultures around the world use altar making as spiritual technology for connecting to Source energy or ancestors. Find what is culturally appropriate for you, and if nothing presents itself, find one sacred item that brings you peace and put it in a corner of your home with a clear written or verbal boundary that no one else but you can touch that item or enter that space. That way, your sacred, slow space is simply infused with your energy. The integrity of this container will support you feeling safe or soothed here, and will support you more frequently accessing it.

I make a daily morning ritual out of making coffee, lighting a candle and sitting at my altar for at least 30min. It sets the tone for the rest of my day to be rooted in the sacred, intentional frequency that I intend (which is usually a prayer for love, compassion, patience, and openness to life.) When shit is hitting the fan, I find that I rely on my altar space exponentially. It's a physical space that can hold me emotionally and mentally without me needing to vomit that energy on other people in my life or engage in harmful behaviors towards myself.

Slowing down is the Sacrament of Safety

Slowing down often signals to ourselves and others a level of care. *I see you. I feel you. I hear you.*

As humans, we tend to learn through contrast. We can begin to cultivate a greater sense of safety by first noticing how we feel around the frequency of fast. How do you feel when someone is speaking a million miles a minute, or you're a passenger in a speeding car? How do you feel when you're having sex with your partner on autopilot, or shoveling food down at your desk because you're "too busy" to take an actual lunch break? Just notice.

This is not to say that moments of fast frequency aren't generative, too. We've all felt the rush and excitement of riding a roller coaster, enjoying that quickie in the back of a car, or running through a park with the zest of a child. However, we can only genuinely enjoy those moments if they are also counteracted with slower moments. Otherwise, the nervous system burns out.

Notice how you feel around someone who truly takes the time to consider their words, or how deeply you can orgasm when you feel your partner following your body cues, one breath at a time. What happens to your breath at a medical appointment when your doctor takes time to answer all your questions and truly get to know you instead of checking off some boxes and prescribing you a pill in a 15min "routine check-up"?

Slowing down helps us to notice where we feel safe, and where we feel unsafe.

This is also important when we consider the experience of discomfort. Discomfort and unsafety are not the same thing. You may feel uncomfortable when having a challenging conversation with someone, this is normal. However, if the both of you are speaking slowly and with neutrality, it feels a lot safer than when voices are raised, tone is defensive and condescending, and words are being spewed so quickly that nobody feels heard. If you grew up in environments where you had to assert yourself in order to get noticed, it can feel like fast is the only way to have a seat at the table.

Conversely, slowing down creates a sensation where everyone feels invited. When we feel invited, there's a sensation of belonging. Not everyone grew up in a home that felt safe, and by slowing down we can create interactions with others and the world around us that begin to re-wire home and belonging as safe places to be, because they are filled with care.

To establish safety with another human being is one of the greatest gifts we can give ourselves and them. Safety creates trust. When we trust someone, we're far more likely to be our true selves around them. To fully embody yourself with another is a far more profound healing than years of therapy, a pill, or some expensive retreat on an island could ever provide.

The Sacrament of listening

When we slow down, we begin to listen to our internal cues, such as how we feel, why we feel that way, and what we need.

It can feel scary to slow down and listen to our internal voice, because we may not like what we hear. It might feel tender at best, or triggering at worst, to sit with the vulnerability of what's actually there.

This sacrament's invitation is not to do anything about what you hear but like many mindfulness practices, simply be a witness to it. When you're present to your internal landscape, instead of ruminating on the past or future-tripping, then you're in a powerful place to make change.

But here's the caveat: *when you're ready to.*

Change cannot be forced, it can only happen when there's a readiness. Sometimes the stakes aren't that high and we're willing to make pretty benign changes. Other times, it takes hitting rock bottom and getting overwhelmingly sick of our own shit before we finally take the hand of our own voice and allow it to lead us home to something healthier. Either way, when we're in the practice of slowing down and truly listening to what's present for us, then it becomes second nature to practice this with others.

How many times are you in conversation with someone and before they've even finished their sentence you've formed a response? We all do it. We all want to be seen. The trick is, we have to see the person in front of us if we want the same favor returned. Listen to what people say, and more importantly, listen to what they don't say. When you consciously slow down your breath in conversation, your body can be more present. In this present, embodied state, you're more apt to pick up on people's non verbal cues and how their words and behaviors make your body feel. When we truly listen and feel listened to, we feel seen, and when we feel seen we feel safe. Safety is the conduit to true vulnerability and vulnerability is the gateway to intimacy. Want a better sex life or working relationship with your boss? Slow down and *listen.*

Mistakes happen when we rush. You're still worthy of Love even when you make mistakes. Because you're worthy of Love, period.

Slowing down is the Sacrament of receiving

Speaking of sex life, Slowing Down is also the sacrament of receiving. Ever notice how when you slow down to take a breath before you eat a bite of food, that food actually tastes better? And conversely, you can eat an entire meal at your desk while pumping out emails and proposals and have no idea what your food actually tasted like? Same principle applies to all 5 senses, including the 6th sense of our intuition or energetic creative capacities. Once a genuine container of safety has been created with a sexual partner, such as specific boundaries or desires being stated and agreed upon, try slowing down certain acts. What was once a routine kiss can feel earth shattering, and additionally what was a fairly mechanical orgasm can blossom into full body waves of pleasure, your pussy dripping wet with trust and joy in a way it never has.

When we slow down to truly take our environment in, our vision becomes sharper and technicolor-bright. We hear nuance where before we heard one-note. We taste and smell quantum flavor profiles, feel new sensation, and can even receive creative inspirations or "hits/downloads," that were blocked before.

There's no way to fuck it up, I promise, as long as your intention to go slow is rooted in kindness and curiosity. In other words, through the sacrament of slowing down, we can access the more of us, the totality of who we are and what we can feel. It puts us directly in touch with our aliveness. From this more whole place, we come home because we can feel what home is not. Sensation isn't a thought, it's rooted in the body; embodiment is the foundation to your homecoming.

Slowing down is the Sacrament we practice
when we realize we're living inside a dream
come true.

No matter how large or small the achievement,
take time to truly savor it, with all 5 senses.
Slowly indulge yourself in the awareness of how
damn good it feels to be living something that
was once just a dream. You made the formless
into form.

Drink. It. IN.

Remember: it gets to be good!

Celibacy in service to receiving

Celibacy, often connected to our sexual life, is more generally a tool for withdrawing from outside distraction in order to receive inside guidance. In other words, to return our energy back to ourselves. When we receive our own energy back, we also become available to receive more in general because we become acutely present to our lives; we're no longer missing the miracles right under our nose.

Through conscious celibacy, we move from frenzy to focus.

Personal anecdote about celibacy: during the writing of this book, I took a personal vow of sexual celibacy. I realized that for years I'd spent much wasted energy on longing, specifically for a beloved. As the book was coming to a close and my vow had been lifted, I realized that, much to my surprise, a practice of celibacy didn't take my longing away. There was no bibbity bobbity boo moment where it all disappeared and I felt lighter. This is because the Truth is that my longing for Love and connection with another human being was never wrong, it is actually the most natural thing I could ever want. Human beings are literally hardwired for it, and if we don't get it, we die. Babies in orphanages physically perish if they're not held or touched frequently; muscles atrophy if they're not used. Adults are no different. The difference about my longing now, as a 36 year old, is that it's not based in a naive or co-dependent need to fill a void, but instead in the ancient acknowledgement of the very purpose I was always meant to fulfill...*union*.

The world wants to keep us separate, but Love, the true frequency of Love, relentlessly advocates for our union; within ourselves, and with everything and everyone we touch. When you've slowed down long enough to come back home to yourself you will no longer be able to ignore your longing. Like a tsunami of energy you will be magnetized to its manifestation, and the Divine will ensure your purification in the process. May the Sacraments be like lighthouses, guiding your way through the tunnel of longing back home.

The Sacrament of rest

So much guilt and shame can come up when we slow down, because we've been taught that productive members of society don't rest, that resting is synonymous with laziness. To the contrary: world-class athletes understand the deep importance of rest as a key facet to their muscle functioning and growth. Same applies emotionally and spiritually in our homecoming process. As we begin to make life changes in the direction of what better supports our body and soul, a lot of energy can get kicked up, especially if some of our life changes trigger other people.

Living an authentic life is not for the faint of heart. It's not easy, but it's honest. In an effort to make your authenticity more sustainable, please rest. The rest is how your body and being integrate the experiences you are having. Otherwise you're just operating on autopilot and are much more likely to return to old unhealthy patterns that overwhelm or sabotage your growth.

Resting can look like a million different things, so trust the internal messages you receive about this. Take a mental health day from work from time to time. Use your lunch hour to eat and then lie down for 15 minutes listening to your favorite relaxing music. Take a vacation and actually turn your phone on airplane mode. Get a massage.

Sleep-in instead of pushing yourself to go to the gym if you're feeling fatigued. The rest will reveal itself.

The slowing down helps us to hear the reveal.

The breath (stress is the thief of health)

We are more stressed than ever, despite having more access to stress relief products and tools. Trauma upon trauma keeps getting layered onto our collective nervous system, so I cannot emphasize enough the importance of your breath.

This is not some woo-woo yoga bullshit, (although I think the ancient mystics really did know what they were doing), this is science. Conscious breathing circulates more oxygen through your system and supports the down regulation of the parasympathetic nervous system. When the nervous system is hijacked, we not only feel like shit but it's very hard to think rationally or be emotionally present and grounded.

In short, stress takes us out of the body, the breath brings us back.

Stress induces a Fight, Flight, Freeze or Fawn response. The breath can help re-direct those primal responses into something healthier. You don't have to do any kind of fancy breathing technique, either. It's truly just about your conscious awareness of your inhale and exhale that help bring you back. Most modern dis-eases are rooted in stress. The more you can slow down where you would normally speed up, the more you're engaging in preventative health care.

Paradox of slowing down to speed up

The muscle memory of doing a million things at once is so ingrained that we tend to experience it as just a "normal part of life." And since our value is predicated on our productivity, our sense of identity is often wrapped up in being busy. All the stories we tell others about how busy we are often garners an unconscious sense of support, validation, approval or belonging from others.

Because our identity is wrapped up in our busyness, it's hard to see that we're often diluting and diffusing our energy. In other words: our busyness makes us less effective at all the things we're busy being busy at.

As such, many projects or tasks get done in half-hearted ways, if they get completed at all. When we take just a moment to slow down, essentially we're energetically calling our energy back to ourselves. This stops the diluting in its tracks, and we gain clear head space and heart space to hear where to appropriately direct our energy.

Conversely, the slowing down often creates spaces to hear the whispers, or internal screams, of the shit that we really need to let go of or delegate to someone else.

Knowing what is of energetic and practical priority enables us to meet each task at hand with greater consciousness, attention, and care. Not only does this feel better when we're doing it, garnering a sense of self-pride, but often other people who take note of how we do what we do begin to see us as more credible and trustworthy. This, not a frazzled mess, is the identity and belonging that will keep us showing up for life.

Ancestral Healing

Slowing down is often an act of ancestral healing. For many of us, our ancestors suffered famines, immigration stories, and deep traumas that caused survival to be at the forefront of their existence. Rest of any kind was seen as a laughable luxury for a lucky few.

I've watched this story play out epigenetically in my own lineage of Irish workhorse patterns. Glorifying the grind instead of uplifting the importance of self-care.

Every time we consciously choose to slow down is a gift, an offering, forward and backwards, to those who came before us who didn't have the privilege to. It's also a transmission and a permission to those yet to come. Slowing down is a declaration that what was once a privilege is now required and respected as technology for our healing, our evolution, and not just our survival, but our thriving.

This is not to say that hard work and effort aren't valuable. We need to move the needle forward in our lives to accomplish things. But through conscious rest, even just one breath, we re-write the pattern of excluding our bodies from the equation and create greater harmony between all aspects of self.

In slowing down, a woman has access to her full self. From
this place, she is a force to be reckoned with.

Personal Story:

Smart women know when to leave things, or people, that no longer serve them. This is the wisdom of Sacrament 1.

At work...

If Sacrament 1 is all about slowing down in order to create spaciousness to hear the Truth, then I can safely say that every crossroads moment of my life where I needed to make a decision about whether to stay or go, involved this Sacrament. Without having known about the Sacraments of the Goddess consciously (yet), I look back on my life to see that every time I left a job, a partner, or a city there was a profound moment of internal slowing down that had to happen first. There were vivid, visceral moments where life was forcing me to listen, for the greater good of myself, and everyone else involved. These moments couldn't be bypassed, they had to be tended to. There was a reckoning, and from that space, miracles could flow.

25

One such moment involved a career choice. I was freshly out of grad school where I studied to become a Drama Therapist (a clinical psychotherapist that specialized in using dramatic or theatrical principles in conjunction with psychotherapeutic tools.) Nobody really knew what drama therapy was, even in San Francisco, but to say I was a "therapist" held both clarity, and power, within a patriarchal system. So, as a fledgling therapist I was not doing the more shamanic, transpersonal aspects of this work that lit me up. I was, in fact, doing the very in-the-trenches community mental health work that paid the bills.

I was a child and family therapist working for an agency in San Francisco that focused on providing services to at-risk youth. I worked in both their residential and outpatient programs. The population was high trauma, and the nature of my work was more that of a crisis worker or social worker. I tried every which way to make it work, even though my gut had been screaming at me from the beginning that something was off. In my experience, life will get louder and louder until we're forced to make the choice of no choice.

On one particularly exhausting day, I was walking through an inner-city elementary school where I was providing services, when I experienced my choice-of-no-choice moment.

It's important to mention that the school employed physical restraint tactics to "manage" children's behavioral outbursts. In other words, young children were being forcibly held by adults under the guise of creating "safety." This was a common and legal mental health intervention. This never sat well with me, especially as most of my clients were young boys of color and the teachers were often white men and women. My extremely empathic self couldn't help but make parallels to the plantation system or today's modern day prison industrial complex, the very real school-to-prison pipeline.

Homecoming

As I walked up to an area close to one of my client's classrooms, I could both hear and see my client being restrained by his teacher. My client, a young black boy, face down on the ground, lying between a doorway, with his teacher standing over him, grasping his hands and feet so the client couldn't move, was crying out.

Did this child have a history of physical violence? Yes. Was this child diagnosed with severe mental illness? Yes. Was this child also the product of chronic and acute trauma? Yes. And now, was this child being retraumatized by the very system that was supposed to "educate" him and keep him "safe?" Yes.

As I watched this scene unfold, my whole body froze. I experienced both a direct and a vicarious trauma, simply witnessing this inhumane scene. As I heard this young boy's cries, I looked to the teacher and other staff to scan for any hint of remorse. Finding none, I felt something happen.

Time and space collapsed in that moment. Time stood still, the ultimate slow down. I could see how harmful and flawed the system was, and would continue to be, long after any change I could implement in it. I could feel every past and parallel lifetime of karma playing out on this field. I could feel how utterly sick the whole scenario made me. And I knew in my bones that I could not in good conscience continue to participate in it. No amount of good, joy, or healing I might be able to provide would outweigh the harm being done. I was not here to change the system from within the system. I was here to recognize that the system was fucked from day one, and the only way I could move forward in integrity was to go create my own system.

27

Children deserve better. The educators, therapists, doctors and facilitators who show up to serve deserve better. Human beings deserve better.

I went to work the next week and put in my notice. I had no idea how I'd pay the bills, and I didn't care. To walk into that school, especially in a position of power with the title "therapist" literally felt like sandpaper to my soul.

The most powerful thing I could do was leave. The most loving thing I could do was let go.

In doing so, I created quite a ripple effect at the agency I worked for: several other therapists left shortly after. We got into this profession to help, not to perpetuate trauma or be so traumatized from the work ourselves that we couldn't show up in service.

To be fair, there are good people on the ground level built for this work. There are incredible community mental health agencies fighting the good fight. This moment woke me up to the knowing that this was simply not my work, and not my fight. I could either resist that and burn myself out in order to prove something, or I could slow down and begin to listen for a better way.

Every time I've slowed down to listen, I've been empowered to make a choice that was far more aligned with my soul, but also with my body. I felt a weight lifted, my health was more vibrant, and I simply felt better in every way after I left that job.

That feeling of Truth and health is a feeling you can't un-feel. It might require more courageous and vulnerable choices upfront, but it always, and I mean always, creates a feeling of wellness in the long run. You, my Queen, are worth the wellness. In every fucking way!

... and at home

Another such moment involving Sacrament 1 involves my love life. Because love and money are really at the core of all our big life decisions, aren't they? More of this will become illuminated in Sacrament 7, but the immediate kernel has to do with red flags.

So, I fell, and fell hard for a beautiful woman while I was in grad school. Perhaps my life was operating at such an intensity in those days that my warp-speed functioning prohibited me from sensing red flags from the get-go. However, it is more accurately true now, upon reflection, and a shit ton of my own personal growth work, that the speed of my life was not the issue. It was a deep desire for belonging, and coinciding fear of abandonment, that was driving the bus of this relationship.

There I was, day in and day out, tending to other people's needs in my professional and academic life, and all I wanted was to come home and have someone other than myself tend to mine, to experience some sort of reciprocity in life. I was holding so much, wasn't there someone who was supposed to hold me?

Now, there were many beautiful moments with my ex-partner. So much love and generosity exchanged. But if I'm honest, there were signs very early on that something wasn't quite right. We were together for almost five years, engaged to be married for over two. Throughout that time, I kept pushing past every internal signal to slow our love train down; I didn't want to have to acknowledge the truth that slowness would have revealed. But then, inevitably, the choice of no-choice arrived.

After a year-long snowball of navigating financial, sexual, health-related, and even addiction issues within the relationship, I found myself one morning waking up from the most viscerally intense dream I'd ever had. It was the beginning of the end. The kind of dream where I felt hunted, in the best way possible.

There *he* was, the strongest, most solid and sexy man I'd ever experienced. He went from moving his hand across my back, to all of a sudden being on top of me. Deeply penetrating, in all the ways. In the dream, I felt the deepest sense of peace, surrender, and simultaneous turn-on of my life. I experienced wave after wave of orgasm, that seemed to bring me back to an ancient re-membering of who I really was, and what I was truly meant for. Visions of a Golden Temple filled with initiatory rites of passage that could only pass through my Holy Grail womb. As my ecstasy echoed through the temple, I felt sure my partner could hear me in waking life.

In what felt like a cosmic moment of climax, I suddenly awoke. Shot straight up in bed! Back on planet Earth, I turned to my left to see my partner fast asleep. Her curly hair resting beautifully upon her cheeks, and in that moment, time and space collapsed, everything stood still, and that same blanket of stillness that fell over me in the school watching that boy being restrained, fell over me in my own bedroom.

I couldn't run. The grief was too loud now. In the core of my core, in the womb of my womb, I knew I could no longer hide from the Truth.

This was not my life. And it hadn't been for a while. I tried so hard to convince myself it was. I truly could not reconcile that I could love someone so much, in fact fall more in love with her throughout the years, and yet simultaneously know I wasn't meant to be with her. How could this happen? Why was this allowed to happen?

"The learning, my dear." Said the Goddess. These tragically beautiful plot twists happen for our own embodied learning. No text book, just the grief and joy of true trial and error.

Homecoming

In the slowing down of that moment I knew everything needed to change, I couldn't un-know that. Although the unraveling of that relationship was messy and hard, at least it was honest. At least I had the courage to liberate myself, and in turn, liberate the both of us to something more True.

Sometimes the acts of service associated with Sacrament 1 are painful initiations that become our greatest call to action. A rising to root into our Truth. And Truth is the only foundation Sovereignty can be built upon. That "good hurt" is always worth the crown at the end. And let's be real, Mary Magdalene didn't hurry the fuck up for anyone. Nor did She throw a tantrum when the church outcast her as a whore. She's been patiently waiting for 2000 years for us to get on board with Love.

Practicing Sacrament 1
Overview

Shadow: Procrastination, stagnation, staying in the gestation phase without ever taking action

Chakra: This sacrament is connected to our Root Chakra. This chakra is located at the base of the spine and radiates the color frequency of red. This chakra is connected to the feet, ankles, and legs; the parts of the body that connect us to the Earth. So, any time you touch or place attention on these parts you are consciously connecting to the wisdom of both this chakra and this sacrament. This chakra connects us to the Earth and earthly resources. It also connects us to our biological lineage or "roots," so connecting to this chakra and sacrament can support our ancestral healing. When out of balance we experience fear. Slowing Down and connecting to this chakra helps to ground and restore a sense of trust & safety within oneself and the environment.

Earth Cycles

Moon phases: The New Moon is typically known as the "dark moon." This is a powerful time of slowing down to go inward, listen for deeper truths or intuitions, and then set intentions and plant seeds for that which you desire to see sprout over the next 6 months.

You can also apply this sacrament to the two week process in between the New and Full Moon each month. If we consciously slow down while working with our intentions, we ensure that no detail goes untended or unnoticed. Our slowing down supports our successful fulfillment, completion or manifestation at the time of the Full Moon.

To practice this Sacrament on the Full Moon supports our capacity to truly savor whatever we have manifested, completed or released at the Full Moon. Slowing down supports our *presence*, no matter how you choose to work with the monthly lunar cycle.

Seasons: This sacrament is typically connected to the Fall and Winter seasons where our bodies naturally slow down to harvest and hibernate. However, I love applying this sacrament to all 4 seasons to support sustainability.

Slowing down supports sustainability in the Spring and Summer seasons where new life is emerging at such a swift pace that we can be prone to burnout simply due to our excitement and joy! Sometimes a hot quickie is fun, but the path of Queendom is all about that slow, sustainable, burn. Oh yeah baby!

Supports

Mantras:

- I am worthy of slowing down
- When I slow down I am connected to my Truth, my pleasure, my power, my_____ (fill in the blank).
- Slowing down supports my ancestral healing.
- Slowing down returns me to the Earth's natural rhythms and cycles. This returns me to my natural rhythms and cycles.
- When I slow down, I call all of my energy back to me.
- Slowing down rewires my body for safety and pleasure.
- Slowing down is my birthright.
- Slowing down is my direct connection to TRUTH.
- Slowing down connects me to the root of who I am.

Divine Feminine allies:

- Hestia or Vesta
- Yuki-Onna
- White Buffalo Calf Woman
- Eirene

Herbal ally: Dandelion

- Dandelion is known as the "Earth nail" and connects us to Mother Earth quickly and powerfully. She is well-known for her abilities to detox our bodies so that we can have a stable and clear foundation for the other Sacraments to flow through.
- This herb can be ingested through teas, tinctures, infused honey and elixirs. However, simply meditating on this herb can bring powerful insight and awareness.

Songs:

- "Threnody" by Goldmund
- "Intention Feat. Morley" by EarthRise SoundSystem
- "Yoga Chill" by Janapriyan Levine
- "How to See the Sun Rise" by Ben Sollee
- "Slow Down" by Skip Marley, H.E.R
- "Slow Down," by The Human Experience, Rohne, Elijah Ray
- "Slow Down" by Scott Orr

Integration tools:

Breath, breath, breath! This is what the ancient yogis have known this whole time. My suggested breathing technique is as follows (but truly, any way you feel called to breathe that supports you accessing more of yourself is great!): inhale through nose, exhale through mouth, making sure to extend the exhale longer than the inhale. Extended exhales are what support the down-regulation of our nervous system and create a state of calm.

Sacred space. Whether it's an entire room to yourself or an altar in a corner of your house, having a dedicated sacred space just for yourself lets your body know there is a safe place to slow down. In this space, you can ground your energy, but also process emotions or ask for higher guidance before moving into the outer world. This is a space of support, strengthening, and celebration of who you are and what your intentions are.

Self-communication. Place one hand on heart, one hand on womb, breathe, then ask yourself "How do I feel? What do I need?" Trust that you know how to answer this for yourself.

Conscious consumption. Prepare food and chew food more slowly, noticing how when you slow down with your food you can savor the flavors more and digest the energy of it more easily

Pause before responding to technology. You are not required to be at everyone's beck and call! Put your phone down, turn the email off, and just take one long breath. This will shift the energy with which you respond, but it will also benefit whoever is on the other end.

Earthing. Place bare feet on the Earth for at least 30 seconds, and leave them there for as long as you wish. Feel yourself give and receive love from Mother Earth. This supports your nervous system and your emotional body to de-stress

Take a walk, meditate, or dance before making a decision. This sounds like the anti-slowing down, but when we engage in embodiment before decision making, we create a sacred pause that gets all of us online, not just our minds. And we all know how our monkey minds and egos would love to run the show!

Practice sexuality more slowly. Introduce more foreplay, make-out, take deep slow breaths to enhance sensation and connection to yourself or your partner. Slowing down in sex also supports boundaries. And let's be honest, when a woman flexes her boundaries in the bedroom it's HOT!

Practice walking or speaking more slowly. Notice the effect this has on your thoughts. When we're able to slow our thoughts, we're able to make more deliberate decisions and express ourselves more authentically. No rushing, no performing required. Slowing down our speech also supports our capacity to more thoughtfully choose our words. Clear, conscious communication deeply enhances a sense of harmony in relationships, whether personal or professional.

Invocations

Prayer:

Divine Mother, help me to know that I am safe to slow down, worthy of slowing down, and inherently know how to slow down with every fiber of my BE-ing.

There is nothing for me to do. Nothing for me to prove. I am exactly where I am meant to BE.

When I slow down, I am met with the Truth of my enoughness, and this ripples out into every facet of my life.

I am enough. I have enough. There will always be enough. And as such, I am forever held in Your grace and protection.

In the slowing down, I remember that I am Loved, and that I AM Love.

I am whole, just as You intelligently designed me to BE.

Thank you for your unwavering divine guidance provided in every moment I slow down long enough to create space for You to enter.

I trust the divinity inherent in slowing down.

Journal prompts:

Writing is such a powerful tool for both insight and integration. As such, I suggest journaling with each Sacrament on a regular basis. You can simply create a dedicated time and sacred space for free writing to see what emerges, or, you can dialogue with the Archetypes and parts of Self suggested below:

How does Slowing Down benefit my: Self, Relationships, Earth AND, what does my Self, Relationships, or Earth know for me about how I can best embody this Sacrament? Where do any of these areas experience resistance to this Sacrament? Where are my blockages and where does it feel easeful to practice this Sacrament?

Sarah Grady, MA

Archetypes: The Divine Feminine archetypes or Triple Goddess energies are broken down into the Maiden, the Mother, and the Crone. Each of these archetypes lives within us no matter our age. However, there are specific seasons where we're more likely to be experiencing these energies more prominently. The Maiden phase is our youthful self, initiated at first menstruation. She often seeks adventure and pleasure, and dances with the energy of seduction and naivety. This phase typically occurs in our 20's. The Mother archetype typically occurs in our 30's and 40's, however, it can be initiated anytime we physically bear children, take part in the raising of children, or are required to assert strong self-care and boundaries. The Crone phase is our older, wise-woman self, generally thought to emerge after menopause, though I personally feel this energy walks with us from birth. The Crone energy is the energy connected to the Mystery, the Cosmos, the Universe, the All. As you work with each of the 7 Sacraments of the Goddess, invite each of these Feminine archetypes to support your journey. Journal for 10 minutes from the perspective of each and see what comes through! Ask each archetype what they know for you about each Sacrament. I guarantee some big gems will come out of this practice!

Sarah Grady, MA

Free write: Your free-write session might include calling-in the frequency of Slowing Down and asking it for guidance. It could include all the reasons you feel unworthy of slowing down or challenged by it (if this is the case, I highly suggest the elemental ritual at the end of this section). Or you might just write, "Slow Down, Slow Way Down" at the top of your page, set a timer for 15 minutes, and then stream-of-consciousness write until the timer goes off. It's always fun to go back and read what came through. Our subconscious has so much to tell us, if we just give it space!

Sarah Grady, MA

Elemental release and reclaim ceremony

This Sacrament is connected to the elements of Fire and Earth. As such, you'll want to gather a candle, a piece of paper and something to write with, and an element of Earth to bring inside your home (i.e. crystal, flower, soil, sand, etc) OR I love doing this ceremony outside in my backyard or any other area where a contained fire pit exists (campgrounds, etc.)

This ceremony is known as a Burn Ceremony. It consists of 3 parts: Release, Forgive, Reclaim.

Release: Light a fire in a safe, contained space. Write on a piece of paper everything you're ready to burn/release/let go of in relation to slowing down. I highly suggest writing down limiting beliefs about how "hard" you think slowing down might be, your beliefs around lack of time or resources to slow down, or any negative messages that were passed down to you through your lineage (especially the maternal side) about slowing down. Write everything down that stands in the way of you fully embracing and embodying this element. You can begin every sentence with, "I let go of the belief that..." There's no right or wrong, just feel your way through this and trust the process.

Once you feel like the list is complete, I suggest reading each item on your list aloud. This externalizes the energy so you're no longer carrying these beliefs inside of you.

After reading each item aloud, toss that paper into the fire (being careful not to burn your precious hands, of course)!

Once the paper has fully burned, extinguish the flame. This energy has now been transmuted by the fire, the element of alchemy, so it can come back to you in the highest and best way.

Forgive: Relight your fire and speak forgiveness into the flame.

Forgive others for projecting their beliefs onto you (this could include family members, society, work, higher education, you name it).

However, it's most important to forgive *yourself* for any and all ways that you have not allowed for slowing down. Forgive yourself for any personal judgment, shame, guilt or worry, and just speak it all into the fire.

Once you feel this process of forgiveness is complete, extinguish the fire once again to seal the energy of this portion of the ceremony.

If you are outside doing this ritual, it can be really helpful to stand barefoot on the Earth, feeling the support of the ground beneath you as you release and forgive.

Reclaim: Last but not least, relight your fire for the final time. This time it is in the frequency of deep reclamation and celebration! Scream, shout, sing, whatever feels nourishing, and declare out loud all the ways in which you are reclaiming your right to Slowing Down and embodying this Sacrament fully.

There's no right or wrong way to do this, so trust what comes through, and have fun! Feel your personal power coursing through your body as you make this declaration to the fire. Be witnessed by the fire and the Earth, as your intentions are now grounded into your being.

You are now self-annointed in Sacrament 1: Slow Down, Slow Way Down.

Homecoming

Feel free to repeat this ritual as many times as you need. We all go through different seasons and cycles of life that are busier than others. It can be easy to forget this sacrament in the flurry of life.

Remember, the Sacraments are a life-long practice. As such, you're not here to perfect them, you're here to give yourself permission to embrace them and receive what they were intended to do: SUPPORT YOU on your path to a Sacred, Sensual, Sovereign life!

Sacrament 2:

Honor Your Body as a Temple

Re-membering

There was a time when we listened to the body and made allyship with its messages. When we honored and cared for it just as we would any sacred object in a holy place of worship.

There was a time when we understood the technology of our sex to be sacred, a holy portal connecting us directly to the Divine.

There was a time when all stages of body development had proper rites of passage and we developed mastery in deciphering how to be at one with these fluctuations, free of shame.

There was a time when the body was cared for, not criticized.

There was a time when there was true reciprocity between our physical bodies and the Earth body of our planet, and in this time women felt safer. All bodies felt safer. Our unborn ancestors felt safer.

Remember this time.

Honor Your Body as a Temple

"The Body is the Soul's Chance to Be Here."

— Meggan Watterson

Your Body is a Temple

Let's get something straight.

Your body is NOT

A burden

An apology

A hot mess

A threat

Too big

Too much

The disease you might be experiencing

Your body is NOT "asking for it"

Your body is NOT a dumping ground for other people's trauma, judgments or opinions.

Your body is NOT weak, damaged or incapable.

Your body IS

A sacred, sacred temple

That IS

YOURS

And YOURS ALONE.

Despite what transgenerational traumas or beliefs were passed down in utero by your mother, and her mother, and the mother of the mother.

Your body is your own.

It is intelligently designed for health, wholeness and vitality.

It is meant to experience deep pleasure and joy.

It is the seat of creation.

It is nothing short of a miracle.

It's the only one you've got,

So first and foremost,

BE KIND.

Homecoming

Kind in thought, kind in word, kind in the way you feed and nourish, kind and discerning about who you let touch and hold and please or bring healing to it.

BE respectful and honoring of its boundaries, limitations and freedoms, and how it interacts with others'.

Be loving

Be joyful

Be wise

But most of all

LISTEN.

Listen to the aches & pains, listen to the warmth, expansion, softening,

listen to the TURN ON, listen to the pleasure, listen to the orgasm of life moving through you.

Listen to the goosebumps.

Listen to the lightening bolt of electricity that shoots up your spine when something is a HOLY HELL YES!

And equally listen for the NO,

(Even if your inner good-girl people-pleaser is horribly uncomfortable with it.)

Listen not just for the obvious and the extreme, but begin to listen for the subtle.

The subtle whispers of the body often hold a treasure trove of information that is waiting for us if we will be patient enough to slow down, ask for guidance, and then LISTEN.

Allyship and Conscious consumption

To honor the body means we first have to form a relationship with it. Not as something to be afraid of or burdensome, but as a friend, or trusted ally.

The body is not here to betray us. Often it is us that betrays the body, usually in exchange for the illusion of love.

To ally with the body means to take time to listen to its messages instead of pushing through, self-medicating, or avoiding because we're afraid of what those messages might be telling us. The body indicates to us all day long. If we're paying attention, then we can heed these indications through our behavior around consumption.

In the West, we are a consumer-based society; we're programmed to consume our reality instead of co-create with it. This is how capitalism functions. As a result, many people are consuming on autopilot without tracking if what they are consuming is helpful or harmful to them. It starts with food and evolves into media, body care products, physical environments, people, and even thought forms and beliefs.

Honoring the body as a temple is about acknowledging the holiness of your physical vessel and consciously consuming accordingly. A woman knows, she just *knows*, when a sexual partner is right for her or not, when a food will inflame her or support her, or whether answering that phone call will enhance or derail her day. We bypass that knowing in an effort to please others and "belong," but we often get burned in the process.

Maybe the messages you get from the body don't always make sense, but you begin to start following them as an experiment to see what happens. When the result of that experiment creates experiences of greater health, joy, stability, and flow in your life you won't be able to help but honor them. You'll feel better and this will ripple and radiate into every aspect of your life.

Did you lose weight, or are you just happy?

In a thin-obsessed culture, current patriarchal compliments often sound like, "You lost weight! You look amazing!" instead of "You're glowing, what's making you so happy these days?"

To be clear, thin does not equal happy.

In a world where everything is energy, so too is food and metabolism. Ever notice how you can eat and exercise the same amount, and for seemingly no good reason your weight fluctuates? That's often because there's something unrelated to diet and exercise impacting your system at large. Stress of something negative, or the blessing of more aligned opportunities, relationships and environments all reflect something in our physical form.

The trick is not to judge what's unfolding in the body. So much easier said than done, but if you can move out of judgment and into curiosity, our relationship to the body becomes less of a place of extremes and more of a ground for daily dialogue. May we learn to root that dialogue in Love and witness what happens as a result.

Prioritize pleasure; the body is not a sin

Let's get something straight, the body is not a sin and neither is sex. The sacred act of sex is how we get created and the body is the alchemy of that creation into form. We need both sex and the body to be here, they are inherent to the process of homecoming. To promote otherwise is to make us all heretical orphans perpetually lost in the land of "not-good-enough."

Seems to me then, that the most loving thing we can do is embrace every fractal of our embodiment as holy. When we prioritize it, instead of condemning or repressing it, we create a vast river of possibility for our healing and our wholeness. We then give others permission to do the same.

By prioritizing our pleasure, we model to the world that our healing doesn't always have to involve our suffering. It also gets to include a bone deep reverence for what turns us on.

The portal of pleasure

Something powerful happens when we engage in our pleasure: we get instantaneously catapulted into the present moment. I'm talking about pleasure in the broad sense here. Think about what happens when you see a sunrise, hear the laughter of a baby or your favorite song come on the radio, what shifts in you when you receive a hug or a kiss, smell fresh coffee brewing or taste the juice of a fresh mango grown in your backyard. Holy moly, we come alive in those moments and we become acutely aware of how delicious it is to be alive!

The sensual becomes a gateway to remembering why we chose to be here in human form. We need these reminders to help lift the burden of ruminating over the past or future-tripping with worry.

When we engage in the portal of pleasure we give ourselves the sacred offering of joy. When faced with the present pleasure of a nourishing meal or dancing to the music that lights us up, something else happens: our priorities come into perspective, we immediately remember what has value for us and what is the shit that we can JUST LET GO.

We've all had those moments. Maybe you just had the best sex of your life or stood beside the ocean of a land you've always wanted to visit and somehow in an instant you realized that losing your job was a blessing in disguise, or that your debt does not define you, or that a past mistake in love was really just another opportunity for you to love yourself more.

We engage in pleasure not as a form of indulgence or escapism, but as a sacred technology for consciously stimulating our senses to be present in the here and now, it's a way of calling ourselves back to ourselves. Pleasure is a portal for coming home.

The technology of beauty

There's a difference between putting on makeup and clothing that we think will garner us love and attention vs. consciously adorning ourselves with things that make us feel beautiful, smell good, and boost our confidence. The latter is a vehicle for outwardly celebrating our inner essence.

Our inner and outer bodies deserve holy celebration. They also deserve the holy reminder of who the fuck we are in the moments when life knocks us down and we forget; sometimes, it literally is that red lipstick or black leather boots that ignite the flame of our homecoming.

Eat the cannoli

This is my personal metaphor for engaging in pleasure. For one, I freaking love cannolis, but they also represent the sweetness of life. During periods of hard work, focus, grief or confusion, I often remind myself to "eat the cannoli" as a way to say "Don't take all this so seriously, Sarah. Take a moment for yourself to come back to the sweetness. The heavier things will be there to pick back up if you really need to."

What is your eat the cannoli moment? Is it walking around your favorite lake, or indulging in a Netflix series? Give yourself permission to fully experience it from time to time, not as something you've earned the right to do, but as a gift you give yourself because you're alive. Period.

Remember, it gets to be good.

Safe touch is the missing nutrient. Start with yourself.

Womb work

The inner temple of a woman's body is her womb. Whether you physically have one or not is irrelevant. If you were born with one, or are transgendered, you still carry the energetic imprint of one.

Inside this temple is both our physical and energetic capacity to create life. Sometimes that life is a baby, but more often than not it's something else. There is no creation that is more important than another.

To honor the body as a temple is to listen to and ally with the inner creative life force inside you that desires to move energy into form. If you are feeling itchy, anxious, or restless in any way, it's often an indication that your creativity is calling.

I invite every woman to begin to have conscious conversations with her womb, or even specifically with parts of her womb, such as her ovaries, to feel for what wants to be birthed in her life. Maybe there's a garden, a delicious dinner that will feed a loved one, a piece of art, or a handwritten letter that will change a friend's day, ready for the attention of her creativity.

When we honor the organic impulse to create from within the body, then what we create is filled with our very essence. This gives a woman a deep sense of pride in her offering to life, it gives her a profound sense of participation in the co-creation of life itself. She then moves from standing on the sidelines of her life to truly living, and this sensation feels like home.

When we give and receive from this place, we amplify a sense of belonging for everyone we touch. If we have experienced pain, disease or trauma in our wombs, it can feel deeply challenging to access this part of us or to practice this Sacrament in general. Go slow. There is no rush in the process of homecoming. Whether it takes you 40 minutes or 40 years to make contact with this part of yourself does not matter. Every woman is on her own unique, sovereign journey. She will feel when she is ready, and when her readiness meets her longing, a miracle will unfold.

Note: there is no right or wrong way to make contact with your womb. It might be a very private experience of self-pleasure, journaling, or taking a hot bath and asking your womb to speak to you. It might also require a village of other women around you, cheering you on when it gets scary (see Sacrament 5.) The Divine Feminine is not here to compete with other women, so give yourself the gift of your own divinely timed experience.

The Mother Wound

We all come from a Mother, and therefore we all come from a womb. When we're gestating inside our mother's womb we're receiving not just the nutrition provided by the food she eats, but also the energetic nutrition of her thoughts, her emotions, the energy of the environments she inhabits, and the energy of other people in those environments.

As such, if a pregnant woman experiences a physical or emotional trauma during her pregnancy that goes unresolved, the baby not only receives the impact of that trauma but maintains the energetic imprint of it. In other words, the baby continues to carry the unresolved pain of the mother.

Both new and ancient wounds get passed down generation to generation through the womb until someone in the lineage decides to heal it. These wounds might be clear and concrete, like healing generations of physical abuse. They might be more abstract, like healing epigenetic patterns linked to poverty, faminine, or war. They might be the decision to heal the pattern of women in the family staying small and polite instead of speaking their truth.

If our mothers haven't consciously done their own healing work, as children we often bear the burden of feeling like we did something wrong. When our mothers get triggered and project their pain onto us through emotional explosions, dismissal, rejection, or narcissism, it can feel easy to internalize it as something we've caused and therefore must fix. The biggest gift mothers can give their children is the gift of their own healing. And children, to let them.

In other words, when you're raised to be a good little girl you think you can, and should, do the healing work for your mother because that will somehow garner you safety and love. But if we're holding their pain, they can't actually heal it. If we consciously, energetically, through our intention and loving boundaries, return their pain to them, they can, in their own way, begin to make peace with it. We then liberate ourselves to do our own work.

Every time a woman takes responsibility for her own experience, she liberates another woman to do the same.

Although vulnerable and uncomfortable at times, it feels better to the body and soul to take responsibility for one's healing journey. When we do, people trust and respect us differently, we create more opportunities for integrity and safety, and we become the love we want to see in the world.

Part of the human condition is suffering. To do our own healing work is not to eradicate suffering, that is impossible, and surely no mother is perfect nor should she be. However, when a mother decides to bring consciousness to what was previously unconscious she promotes a balancing of the scales, she declares to herself and her unborn child that right alongside suffering there also gets to be joy, peace, love, and harmony. She declares that it gets to be good.

Imagine how different the world would be if we knew that we were inherently born good? We'd spend a lot less time striving to prove that goodness to unhealed people, and instead radiate it out to create more goodness. That kind of world isn't impossible, it's literally just a choice we make, in the body, one woman at a time.

Queens create their own standards of beauty

Move accordingly, be the audacious embodiment of your unique essence in every room you walk into. And be sure to celebrate the beauty of every other woman around you, too, even when her attitude presents as ugly.

Remember how painful it feels to not know your own worth, hold compassion in your heart, and then lift her crown for her just once, so she might have the courage to toss out society's standards and lift it on her own someday.

Stop judging other women's bodies and start deepening
the relationship with your own.

Your body is NOT available as a topic of conversation

Not at family functions. Not in friend circles. Not in professional realms. Not in any case unless there is serious concern for health reasons. *Your body is not a topic of conversation.*

Capital Culture

There's a reason why the self-care industry is a multi billion dollar industry. Capitalism benefits from your self-hatred. Capitalistic culture profits off our bodies being used for production, it profits off of pointing out our "imperfections" and then sells us products and services to rid us of them.

Capitalism doesn't profit from our self-love. Notice I didn't say self-care, which has become a trendy smoke screen obscuring the same old dangling carrot routine. "Self-care" is now just another item on Wonder Woman's endless to-do list that she must perform perfectly, or suffer shame, blame, and ostracization, all the while unfairly comparing herself and her self-care efforts to those of other women.

In other words, not only are we expected to do it all (backwards and in heels), but if we're not radiating vibrant, holistic wellness while we do it, we are told we have failed at self-care and prescribed more products and services to treat our symptoms. Once again women have accepted the blame for a system that has failed us, and the vicious patriarchal cycle of charging us for the "fix" continues.

The truth is, no amount of bath products, journals or expensive candles will generate SELF-LOVE. Self-love is an inwardly-cultivated knowing, something a woman claims when she re-members she was born worthy. When self-love is present for a woman, she needs nothing but the gift of her own essence.

Self-love is a CHOICE a woman consciously chooses to make. Over time, the muscle memory of self-love over self-hatred becomes strong enough to be the overriding commentary in a woman's self-talk internal voice, and she can't help but radiate that out into the world. And we all know that THAT is universally attractive, and has nothing to do with shape, size, race, sexuality, gender expression, language, or socio-economic status.

Despite living in a fat-phobic culture, we've all had the experience of being around a large, full-bodied woman who just OOZES self-love, just rocks it, and incites and encourages our own self-love just by being in her presence.

How many times have you not worn something, or shied away from doing something, because you didn't think you had the body for it? Then you see someone 3x larger than you or clumsier doing the very thing you told yourself you couldn't, and realize, well shit, I guess I have a choice. I can choose to see my body the way I know it to be (as powerful, as capable, as worthy), or the way I fear others might.

The technology of patriarchy has often expressed itself as men who feel threatened by women's fullness and power to create life, so they see the female form as a threat. But it has also shown up in the way women attempt to control their bodies, internalizing the messages of patriarchy. It can be scary to own our fullness in a world that programs us to associate smallness with safety and belonging.

Queen, your body is a miracle, period. All bodies are miracles. Let's choose to start moving in the world that way. When we do, we give capital culture the boot(y), and create a deep movement of Love in its place.

No more leaking your energy

Think about how much of your precious life force energy you waste on a daily basis in hating your body:

• Wishing it looked different, smelled different, moved differently, etc.

• Suffering through yo-yo fad diets and extreme forms of exercise, when you could simply slow down, get quiet, and then ask your body what she actually needs to function optimally.

• Recovering from substances that momentarily numb or soothe, but ultimately never serve.

• Trying to calculate what time of day it's safe to walk, and where, and how to walk, and what to wear, just so you can potentially reduce the risk of sexual assault?

If we lived in a society that honored every body, not just women's bodies, as a temple, as a sacred entity, would any of us have to leak our energy like this?

We wish that culture would change first and then we could begin the work of adapting to that healing shift. But it just doesn't work that way. Change happens from the inside out, and we have to be the change we want to see in the world.

By consciously prioritizing pleasure, women become fortified with greater endurance and joy on the road to that change.

Feel for boundaries

She may not be able to articulate it with words, but a woman always knows in her body when something is aligned for her or not. The body is the first place to experience and express our boundaries. It might not make logical sense, but the body can energetically track when a person, environment, or opportunity will be generative or harmful.

We slow down in Sacrament 1 so we can begin to cultivate our listening skills. What we are listening for are the messages being communicated by the body; that ancient wise-woman way of speaking with our Soul through the physical form.

When we honor the body as a temple, what we're really doing is treating its form and its communication with due respect, the way we would with a dear friend. Sacrament 2 is all about feeling for the boundary and getting curious as to why something feels right for us or not. No action is required, just feeling.

Body Sovereignty

Your body is the one and only true home you'll ever have. As such, every cell and particle that makes up you is sacred, and it is yours. Your body is not your partner's, your family's, the government's or any institution's. It is yours. When a woman remembers and reclaims this Truth everything, and I mean everything, in her life changes.

Homecoming

A woman who loves her body is a dangerous woman.

Follow the feeling

You don't have to make sweeping life changes to honor this, but one thing I know for sure is that once you feel something in the body, you can't un-feel it.

You can't fuck with feeling. Once you wake up, you can't fall back asleep. So as all this talk about diving deep into the wisdom and sensation of your body might be terrifying, trust that there's no one right or wrong way to do it, trust that you get to be in the driver's seat of your own experience, titrating your experience in a way that feels good to your system (especially depending on your trauma history, and we ALL have experienced trauma, so be kind to your body and go as slow or fast as you need).

One way of staying with your body and its messages is to practice the art of curiosity. When we lean into life with curiosity we instantly reduce our judgment or fear about something. Get curious and when you do, you'll begin to witness the breadcrumbs about how your body, and your life, are working in your favor.

Lastly, **be open to change.** We are in a constant state of cellular death and rebirth, the body regenerating new cellular structures every 72hrs. As such, your taste buds are going to change, when and how and why you move will shift, what brings you pleasure and how you experience pain will morph. Who you're attracted to, what climate feels generative to live in, your personal style and way of adorning and caring for your body, will all change. Your libido and experience of desire in your womb and your heart will shift. Your pace will quicken or slow at times. Your ticklish toes may give way to an even more ticklish pussy, depending on where you are in your monthly cycle. Your body temperature and emotional temperature may dance like Fred Astaire. Even as Winter turns to Spring, don't forget the quantum power of REST.

My prayer is that we collectively support each other in the ALLOWING of those shifts instead of resisting them with botox, plastic surgery, and starving ourselves of the food or experiences our bodies truly need to thrive. That being said, as we established above, your body is YOURS. So get the botox or the plastic surgery or tattoo if that's what will bring you genuine JOY.

But first, Sacrament 1, Slow Down. In the slow still space of your own body only you can filter out society's voice and register the Truth of your own.

And don't forget: *eat the cannoli!*

Personal Story:

The body is the holy grail of all you need to know. All that is required is the safety and willingness to remember this.

After I left my life as a vegetarian lesbian in the Bay Area, I moved to Asheville, NC. The mountains of Appalachia pulled me in like a tractor beam, as it does for many who are ready for Her initiations. The choice of no-choice was that I *had to* move there. Although I'd hoped my move was to be more of a settling, it ended up being just one year. A year of deep healing.

Asheville is quite the little energy vortex of a town, built on a bed of quartz crystal, and high in spiritual bypassing of every sort. For me, the healing I received there was an absolute embodied one.

As a recovering therapist, I decided to work at a non-profit yoga center coordinating their healing arts center and attending yoga teacher training. This was its own initiation into the wolf in sheep's clothing of narcissism cloaked in spirituality, to be sure, but that's a story for another day and another sacrament. For now, I bow in deep gratitude for the absolute portal this place was in the community and in my own abundant personal growth. Every day, the most magical misfits were placed on my path; every day a new sign or synchronicity leading me onto the next leg of my healing journey, much like my time at Terra's Temple.

One such person was Jackie, a kindred spirit of a woman who was an avid yogi, but also a volunteer in our thrift store. We immediately struck up cosmic conversation with each other one day when she disclosed that she was about to travel abroad to attend a tantric massage training. As a sacred sexual scorpio woman this made every hair on my body stand up. As did the next sentence that came out of her mouth, "So when I return to Asheville I'll need clients to practice on. Would you at all be interested in this?" Would I at all be interested, are you kidding me? Bitch, massage me every day for the rest of my life PA-LEASE!!!! The temple of my body had been a dry fucking well for years, even in a commited relationship with my ex-partner. So, tantric or not, touch me NOW!

A couple months later, there I was, lying naked on this woman's floor, like ya do, breathing deeply and laughing at the wonder of my life. After an hour on my belly, allowing my back body to receive deeply, Jackie directed me to turn over. When I arrived in this new position, she asked if I would like to receive the *internal work*. Meaning, she would insert her fingers into my vagina and connect with my tissues from the inside. Girl, I'm in, I'm all in, so put your fucking gloves on and make my pussy sing!

This was not some hot porn star moment of my life, although aspects were certainly entertaining. No, *this* was the moment that shattered me into a million fucking pieces. Jackie very lovingly, and with the utmost of safety and boundaries proceeded to put gloves on and insert her fingers into my vagina. She slowly moved around all 4 quadrants of my womb, making conscious contact with all parts of me, instructing me throughout to stay present and focused on my breath. I was also encouraged to allow any emotions that came up to just flow without judging or labeling them.

I felt my whole body relax, perhaps fully for the first time in my life. There was a rush of healing and peace that flooded me, and a bittersweet awareness; shouldn't we all experience such safe and sacred touch from the very beginning? How different would the world be if our bodies were honored with such loving tender care, for the holy temples they really are?

And then it happened.

Jackie began to quicken her penetrative speed and began touching parts of my womb that had never been touched before, not by myself, and certainly not by a partner. I could feel myself preparing, could feel a bracing coming on, perhaps for a depth of pleasure that might just explode every cell and particle. My breath quickened, my heart expanded, my back began to arch...

Sometimes I wish orgasmic pleasure is what would've happened, but instead, Jackie hit such a deep place inside that everything in my whole body and being broke down, or perhaps, broke open. In a flash, I sprung up from the massage table and doubled over, screaming the only thing my voice could manage to utter:

"Will anyone ever love me?!"

Like a mantra on repeat at the altar of a holy deity, these were the only words I could recognize as True. I sobbed, like a newborn baby wails during delivery. I had been delivered, and Jackie was my midwife. She held me and wiped away my tears as I tried to figure out what this strange new world was.

Will anyone ever love me?

It was the most ancient ache my Soul had been questioning, lifetime after lifetime. Here I was, confronted with this question yet again. It was also the most recurring ache of my 32 year old body, which had never known true, unconditional love and safety.

I knew in that moment that I had been delivered into my next sacred assignment: radical self-love. How could I know if anyone outside of me would ever truly love me, if I didn't give that love to me first?

I thought self-love is what I'd been practicing all these years, but was that really true? In this moment, I understood that my body was begging me to write my own love story so I would never again have to ask that question.

It was from that moment on I decided to practice the 7 Sacraments of the Goddess. To honor my body as a temple always, and in all ways. To deeply listen to her signs, signals and messages, and then to actually follow through with actions that honored those sacred communications. To let my body lead me to the true, lasting Love within, again, and again, and again, just as Mary Magdalene had taught. This was my mission.

I give thanks every day to my womb, and the contract I had with Jackie to access my temple's message with so much safety and sanctity. I will say that, over the years, practicing this sacrament has often been the experience of two steps forward, one step back, but I am clear this journey is not about perfection, it is about the Love of permission, and knowing that that is enough. In fact, it is heroic.

Practicing Sacrament 2
Overview

Shadow: Over indulgence, hyper self-care, narcissism, overactive feminine energy and underdeveloped masculine energy, rigidity around boundaries which can lead to never crossing thresholds into that which would empower us.

Chakra: This Sacrament is connected to the 2nd Chakra, located just below the navel. This chakra radiates a beautiful frequency of orange. This chakra and sacrament is connected to your womb. Whether male or female, we all carry a womb, be it physically or energetically. Your hips, glutes, and entire pelvic bowl are included in this chakra. Working with this chakra is our direct connection to our creativity, sexuality, sensuality, money, emotions, and feeling for what our boundaries are. We have to feel them first before asserting them with our 3rd Chakra. Working with this chakra helps us to feel the messages of our body so that we can clearly communicate or take action on those messages in the upper chakras. Working with this chakra supports balanced expression and experience of our life force energy and pleasure so we can fully enjoy our embodied experience free of guilt and shame.

Earth Cycles

Moon phases: If you are a woman who bleeds a monthly menstrual cycle, it can be a powerful practice to track whether you typically bleed on the New Moon or the Full Moon (and to notice if/when this changes.) As you sync up your personal moon cycle to the larger lunar cycles, you'll begin to learn what your body is telling you about what it needs.

Bleeding on the new moon can often be the body's intuitive call for more inward-turning, to support you from burnout and nourish you with greater incubative cycles.

Bleeding with the full moon can signify that your body is currently releasing or completing major cycles and patterns, either emotionally, relationally or within your own physical health.

At the time of the New Moon, how can you nourish and support your body? At the time of the Full Moon, how can you honor your body's fullest expression?

Practice Sacrament 1 first to create space for listening, then let the temple of your body communicate the answers to you through visions you receive, synchronicities that appear, or internal voices whispering messages of encouragement. Your energy levels will always be a great indicator of where to start your honoring process.

Seasons: Honoring your body as a temple is a 4 seasons kinda practice...24/7, 365, Queen!

Each season will present you with new information about how to honor your body through diet, nutrition, hydration, movement, body-work, skin care, and play! Honoring can sound heavy, but actually it's a joyful act of devotion. So follow your body's intuition and enjoy the process!

Supports

Mantras:

- My body is a sacred vessel.
- My body is intelligent.
- I listen to my body, and my body listens to me.
- My sexuality is sacred, not a sin.
- Sex is my sovereign rite.
- My sensuality connects me to the world around me.
- My sensuality is my gateway to aliveness.
- I create my own standard of beauty.
- No matter how my body looks or feels, I am always worthy of LOVE.
- When I honor my body as a temple, I teach other people how to treat me.
- When I honor me, others honor me without question.
- I dictate what substances and energies enter my body. My boundaries are sacred.
- I listen to my body's messages as I would a sacred omen or divine message from God.
- My body is brilliant, and I trust it without question. Its messages lead me into greater health, wholeness, pleasure and joy. To be embodied is my greatest accomplishment.

Divine Feminine allies:

- Aphrodite
- Oshun
- Lakshmi
- Brigid

- Yemaya

Herbal ally: Jasmine

- Jasmine is *the* plant of sacred and healthy sexuality. Her exquisite aroma commands our presence, uplifting moods and calming the central nervous system for our highest pleasure.
- This herb can be ingested through teas, tinctures, flower essences, infused honey and elixirs. It can also be topically applied in hydrosol mists or body sprays. However, simply meditating on this herb can bring powerful insight and awareness.

Songs:

- "Queen" by Jesse J
- "Dance Naked Under Palmtrees" by Mo'Horizons
- "Recovery Music" by Osunlade, Mike Steva
- "Goddess Code" by Lizzie Jeff
- "Poetry: How does it feel?" by Akua Naru
- "In My Womb" by Scarlet Crow
- "Woman" by Amber Lily
- "Mary Magdalene" by Meshell Ndegeocello

Integration tools:

Somatic tracking: Slow down, breathe, notice a physical sensation or symptom in the body. Instead of beating yourself up for it, get *curious*. Ask the body what this sensation or symptom is trying to communicate (i.e is the pit in your stomach a warning sign? Is the rash on your skin a sign of inner inflammation or anger/grief about something?) It's usually connected to an emotion or pattern that is asking for your attention.

Food gratitude: Pray over your food or send Reiki to it before consuming it. Cook it with love and intention. Go slow enough to actually taste it. What do you notice?

Exercise: Reframe exercise not as something you do to lose weight, but something you do to feel powerful, strong, or free!

Muscle testing! Otherwise known as applied kinesiology, this is the process of using your body as a pendulum or tuning fork to indicate what is generative or not for your body. Remember, you always have free will choice. So even if your body indicates a YES/NO, you still get to decide what choice you make. You're the QUEEN. Always.

Prioritize pleasure! Take yourself on a date to your favorite cafe or restaurant. Eat foods that bring you JOY. Sacred touch, etc.

Mindful self-anointment. Take the time to research and buy products that honor your body, and the Earth: chemical free, ethically sourced products, and/or products made with your favorite scent that make you feel like a Queen! Mindfully anoint yourself with these products as a way to sensually bring you into the present moment. This is not selfish, this is self-celebration!

Water worship. The element of Water is deeply connected to this Sacrament: take regular salt baths, hot showers, and swims, hydrate with spring water (which contains nutrients and minerals absent in distilled, filtered, or "purified" water) whenever possible, and pray over your water before you drink it.

Adornment! Channel your inner little girl and play dress-up. Curating our wardrobe, jewelry, and other forms of adornment is a SACRED act of self-love! When we wear things that make us feel beautiful or powerful, we act accordingly, and then the world responds accordingly. You magnetize your desires through these pleasurable acts that we took for granted as children!

Boundaries. Practice saying YES only when it's a Holy HELL YES. If your body indicates it's not quite a yes, it's either a NO, or you need more time/information. This goes for energy, food, relationships, physical environments. Trust your body to give you the cues. And know that this changes. Maybe one day a certain space feels like a yes, but the next week it's a no. TRUST WHAT YOUR BODY TELLS YOU. You are being guided and protected in ways you can't understand yet.

Chronic Illness: This one can be really tricky. Navigating chronic illness can bring up all our shit! From fear, guilt, shame, worry, self-doubt and impatience. This is when I go into Shadow Dance. Although this is just one portion of a Qoya class, I'll often take 3 or 4 songs to dance with my shadow and ask Her what She knows for me today. By inviting our shadow in as a dance partner we learn how to befriend our fear, worry, doubt, etc. and see it as a messenger. Instead of feeling like our body is betraying us, we learn how to become an ally to it. The healing journey is non-linear, and as such, is divinely feminine in its nature.

Body gratitude: Spend time in the mirror and thank your body for ALL it does. State out loud to yourself the MIRACLE that your body is. Affirm that your body is your HOME.

PLAY! PLAY! PLAY!!!!!!! For the love of God/Goddess: PLAY!!!!! Your body will always thank you!

WOMB WORK. This means everything from tracking your menstrual cycles, to cleansing your womb physically and energetically in ways that feel generative to you, to regularly dialoguing with your womb (and all Her parts) to ask what she needs for optimal health and well-being, as well as how She wishes to support your overall health and well-being (which includes physical, emotional, spiritual, and energetic health). Honoring Your Body as a Temple can also include honest conversations with yourself and your sexual partners about conscious conception, hormonal support, sexual history, and sexual preferences. It's YOUR body and no one else's, and your womb is an oracle of information for how to honor it. She will communicate to you through physical sensations and symptoms, but also inner visions and intuitions—that "gut knowing," but just a little lower and deeper than the gut you usually think of.

*A word on trauma: We have all experienced trauma in the body. Depending on your personal experience of trauma, this Sacrament could be quite challenging or vulnerable. This is okay and to be expected. Go slow, be gentle on yourself, remember you literally have your entire life to be in relationship with the body, and calibrate your healing experience as you need so you don't get overwhelmed. Always follow your impulse to seek out trauma-informed professionals to support your process.

Invocations

Prayer:

Divine Mother, thank you for the gift of this human body.

Thank you for the miracle that is every cell and particle, functioning without me even having to think about it.

You help me to remember every day that, because I am wrapped in skin, I am perfect and worthy in every way.

I ask for Your guidance to help me Honor My Body as a Temple. To care for it, inside and out, the way I would a sacred place of worship. I pray for the patience to listen to its messages.

The respect to honor its boundaries and limitations. And the gratitude for all the movement, functioning, and pleasure it affords me.

I pray to release the concept of my body as a burden or something to be changed, and to receive the re-membering that my body is the holy house in which my Soul resides.

This body is a gift. This life is a gift. Every challenge is an opportunity to resurrect, like a Phoenix rises from the ashes, again, and again, and again so I might know the true meaning of Love.

Journal prompts:

Self, Relationships, Earth

Homecoming

Maiden, Mother, Crone

Homecoming

Free write

Sarah Grady, MA

Elemental release and reclaim ceremony:

This Sacrament is connected to the elements of Fire and Water. As such, gather a candle, a piece of paper and something to write with, and an element of water such as a bowl or your favorite drinking vessel full of water, and/or a natural body of water.

Release: Just as we did in the Sacrament 1 ritual, write down all the limiting beliefs you have around your body. All the messages you've received from society, your family system, or your own inner critic.

This is often a very intense topic for women because of our deep patriarchal wounding. Take your time with this, go slow, both write and speak aloud all that you're releasing to the fire, and know that it may take several burn ceremonies until you begin to feel these negative beliefs and energies leaving your system. That is OK. We're undoing thousands of years of conditioning. This process is allowed to be messy, emotional, and anything you need it to be.

Forgive: Once you've properly burned your list or verbally released limiting beliefs into the fire, it's important to invoke forgiveness. Water is the element connected to our emotional body, and it's also connected to healing, soothing, cleansing and releasing. As such, water is a powerful element to work with when we need to forgive ourselves or others.

Just as you spoke into the fire, I invite you to speak your prayer for forgiveness to the water. The vibration of our words are known to change the molecules of water. As such, either declaring forgiveness to the water, or praying for support in learning how to forgive self or other, literally creates an elixir of "forgiveness water."

In this ritual you may want to forgive yourself for all the times you betrayed your body in exchange for love, belonging, safety, etc. You may also want to forgive your mother, your ancestors or society for any of the messages around body image they passed down to you. Trust that whatever comes up is necessary.

You can always repeat this ritual as needed. Once you sense internal completion with this part of the ritual either drink a bit of the water you just spoke into, or wash yourself with it. This literally integrates the frequency of water into your cells for embodied integration.

Reclaim: The completion of Sacrament 2's Self-Anointing is Baptism, a full cleansing and washing away of all past energies related to your body. If you have access to a body of water (hot bath, lake, river, ocean, etc.) I highly suggest fully submerging your body. Otherwise, take the water you used for Forgiveness, and pour it over your head.

In this Baptism, you become reborn, declare a clean slate of energy with your body, and reclaim it as yours alone. From this clean slate, you now get to program your thoughts and beliefs about your body in a way that nourishes and supports your highest health and wholeness, physically, emotionally, energetically and genetically (yes, you declaring a healthy relationship with your body ripples throughout your ancestral line to heal any issues related to embodiment).

Sacrament 3:

No apologies

Re-membering

There was a time when women walked the Earth and unapologetically took up space.

There was a time when women took their seat, fully throned, and villages called them The Oracle, The Medicine Woman, The Seer, The Mother, The Creatrix.

There was a time when women were the drummers, the shamans, the landowners and leaders of communities.

There was a time when women spoke, and people listened. There was a time when women said yes or no, and people listened.

Remember this time.

No Apologies

"He who dares not offend cannot be honest."

— Thomas Paine

Beautiful woman, aside from slowing down, this sacrament is probably the hardest one to put into practice. It is hardwired into our DNA to be a "good little girl," to behave "like a lady," and "keep the peace" at all costs.

Let's be clear, there is a grave cost, and it's not other people's sense of safety or comfort, it's our Soul's.

We have been socialized to not just place other people's power at a higher level than our own, but to actually honor their entire experience of life before our own. This results in our chronic state of apology, simply for existing.

How many times in one grocery store outing do you apologize just for walking down an aisle when someone else is there? How many times do you minimize your feelings about a situation so other people don't judge you as "crazy," "too big," or "too much?" How many times do you minimize your pain so other people don't have to carry the perceived "burden" of taking care of you? How many times do you minimize your need for support? Your desire? Your opinion? Your knowing? Your intelligence? Your voice? Your talent? Your pleasure? Your body? Your wealth or your poverty? Your dreams? JUST TO MAKE OTHER PEOPLE COMFORTABLE???

Sister, this has got to stop.

It's not your fault: you were trained at a high level to learn how to stay safe and get your very basic needs met this way. Often by the woman who brought you into the world, and often for good reason. It's called collective trauma. Transgenerational trauma. Wars. Witch hunts. Forced hysterectomies. Forced lobotomies. Sexual abuse. Abuse of all kinds. Survival. For all the women who came before us, apologies often meant the difference between dying and surviving.

Honor it all, give deep thanks and respect to your ancestors who didn't know better or literally had no choice. You wouldn't be here if they hadn't survived those moments. Standing up for ourselves or taking up space doesn't make us a bad ancestor. We honor our ancestors by living the fullest expression of ourselves because they couldn't. We heal past generations by making the empowered choices they never had.

Wolf in Sheep's Clothing, Take off the Mask of Manipulation:

We are all born wild. We are all born wolves. As wolves, we have a keen connection to our instincts and intuition. As wolves, we KNOW things, in that unshakeable, embodied way. And this is threatening. Not to other wolves, of course, but to the cowardly systems that indoctrinate us into sheep-dom so we can be controlled.

When a woman knows something, she can't un-know it. Even if she has played sheep for 60yrs of her life, she will hit a tipping point of grief that she can no longer cage, and she will wake up to the wild beauty of who she really is. From this place, she will begin to change. You might not notice it at first, but eventually, every room she walks into will feel a molecular shift. She will be so fully committed to Self, and this self-commitment will be the lock and key to the treasure trove of finally being met that she has longed for all this time. Not just met in love, but in every way. The Universe loves clarity, and I don't know anything more clear than a human being radically committed to being fully, wholly, and completely THEMSELVES.

Before we can return to our innate nature, however, we must first acknowledge our engagement in the wolf in sheep's clothing paradigm.

It's a bit of a catch 22. Society trains women to apologize for every little move they make, which inherently sends the message to women, "Be a good girl at all costs." When stuffing our truth down becomes too hard to do, women learn how to manipulate people or situations, in covert or overt ways, in order to get our needs met, stay safe, maintain the illusion of love or belonging, and keep the peace. Because we're not authentically being ourselves, we often unconsciously attract others steeped in falsehoods, as well. This can frequently come in the form of feeling duped or betrayed by someone who turns out not to be who they said they were. It can leave us feeling shaken, stupid, or stuck in a victimhood mentality. The inner dialogue can often sound like, "But I'm a smart woman, how did I let this happen to me?"

Something miraculous happens, however, when we start to own the parts of ourselves that we keep hidden out of fear that we won't be loved or safe; we liberate those parts to have a seat at the table in our wholeness. We sit with them and listen to their messages, and their medicine. We start asking for what we need, and believe we're worthy of receiving it.

Slowly but surely, over time we inhabit more of our wild, organic nature, the self that needs no deprecation or false filter to belong. We inhabit our sense of home and others who do the same find us. Your point of attraction shifts. Safe in the harbor of home, you're emboldened to keep expressing yourself with the people and places that feel like home. You take more risks, you follow your intuition, you dare to dream a bigger dream. You run wildly in the opposite direction of red flags and howl for protection when need be.

Being the wolf becomes the only honest option. No masks allowed.

Your radiance doesn't have to be loud: No apologies is the sacrament of understanding your power. When you're connected to your power, you don't need to flip and flail to get others to notice you. There's no begging, convincing, or endless social media posts to prove yourself. You just are. You don't have to be the bonfire, you can be the single flame and know how radically enough that is.

The world doesn't need your politeness, it needs your BRAVERY AND BOLDNESS. But most of all, it needs your *honesty*. The only way you can truly get honest or real or clear with yourself is by slowing down long enough to actually hear the voice of your Soul.

Once you practice the first sacrament enough that it becomes ritual, it will facilitate your capacity to embody this third sacrament. You will begin to feel on a cellular level how good it feels to no longer apologize for being here. Once you have felt this, it will feel crippling to go back to the pattern of constantly dimming your own light.

Now, none of us will be perfect at this. Perfection is not the goal, self-worth is the goal. And with each passing day of honoring and owning your self-worth and respect you begin the work of eradicating the "good girl" and allowing the "wise woman" to rise and SHINE.

Like, REALLY shine.

And yes, you are wise. Your wisdom has been gained through experience. Honor it. It's a bridge, sometimes even a life raft, for those around you. Do not apologize for it. Radiate it.

I get it, apologizing is often the much easier route. Particularly when we sense that the person in front of us will not be able to hold, let alone celebrate or honor your lack of apology.

Simply, Your shining will surely piss some people off. This is a good thing. You will know you're on the right track when people start to push back on your lack of apologizing. People will start to project their unprocessed grief, anger, rage, disappointment, and envy on you. They may say things like, "This is so unlike you, what's gotten into you, why are you being like this, I want the old you back, why are you doing this when you could be making the 'smart' decision?"

Your growth will shine a light on other people's fear of their own growth. It will illuminate where they have lacked boundaries or courage or self-respect. It will challenge them to slow down and get honest with themselves. It will challenge them, wake up, make scary, vulnerable, intimate decisions; to really live. None of this is your job or obligation to respond to. Learn how to piss the right people off (hint: they will be the ones to ultimately join you on the sacramental path of evolution and authenticity). Let the rest fall where they may.

The world thinks it wants us to tap dance and tip-toe around in co-dependent patterns that don't rock the boat; of outsourcing instead of in-sourcing ourselves. Ultimately, however, our embodied declaration of worth is far more inspiring. It's also more healing. And healing is what the world needs.

When you stop apologizing, you model to others not only how to shift into self-worth, but that they get to, as well. You give everyone else around you a giant permission slip to be fully who they are. And this creates the experience of people feeling seen, heard, celebrated. This in turn creates more love. People are no longer acting from a place of woundedness and attention-seeking, but instead from a place of greater peace and self-belonging. Quite literally, this is how we create peace on Earth.

"No" is a complete sentence. Stop cloaking your NO in an explanation. Explaining yourself is apologizing for yourself.

"I'm not available" is also a complete sentence. Use it as a response, with no other explanation, and see how edgy, liberating, perhaps scary but really fucking awesome THAT feels! Then do it again.

If it's not a HELL YES, it's a NO

You owe no one an explanation of why your yes is a yes and your no is a no, least of all yourself. Your YES and NO just is, it's not up for debate.

Assertion of boundaries

If Sacrament 2 is the place we begin to feel for our boundaries, Sacrament 3 is the place of asserting them, without apology. Boundaries create clarity. When we stop apologizing and learn how to state our wants, needs or feelings clearly, we create extremely clear containers for ourselves and others to organize around.

We also stop expecting people to read our minds or meet our unarticulated expectations that we were too afraid to state. **When people know where you stand, they know how to stand with you.**

That doesn't always mean that we get those wants or needs met, but it does mean we maintain our integrity in the process. And that is everything.

The constant commitment to strive for acknowledging and acting from our integrity creates an unshakeable sense of self. This rooted self can ride the waves of disappointment, crises, mistakes, or betrayal with far more grace and compassion because it doesn't feel guilty or ashamed for what life is presenting. You know your inherent "goodness" and "worthiness," regardless of life circumstances. You take things less personally and dance with life in greater neutrality. Compassion towards self and other creates an alchemical space for healing and transformation, and even miracles, if we allow it.

Boundaries are meant to create that which is life-affirming. In other words, boundaries create a space for yourself and another to move in a way that is supportive, not destructive. When you struggle to set a boundary, or to even know what boundary needs to be set, a helpful practice can be calling all of your power back to you. This sacrament is connected to our third chakra, our solar plexus, the energetic center for our sense of identity and autonomy in the world. It's the place of SHINING! It's also the place of our personal power.

If we're in a constant state of apologizing, we are inherently leaking our energy and power to the person/place/situation we're apologizing to. Catch yourself when you're spiraling, feeling foggy, or you physically feel a contraction in your solar plexus (or diaphragm), this might be a signal to say out loud, "I call all of my power back to me, now!" It's really that simple. Then visualize your solar plexus fully intact, bright, shining yellow or gold, and warm-fire is the element attached to this sacrament, so warm yourself up, burn away any doubts or fears, and then rise like the phoenix from the ashes with your clear YES or your NO-without an ounce of apology.

You are not responsible for other people's emotional reactions

Not when you're speaking your Truth, not when you're asserting a boundary, not when you're in a mood they don't like, or when you're brimming with joy and it shines a light on their lack thereof. You are not responsible for other people's emotions. Period. So stop cloaking your clarity in apologies.

Acknowledgement is not apology

There's a difference between apologizing and acknowledging. Apologizing for things that we don't need to perpetuates a caretaking and codependency model (a savior or martyr complex). Acknowledging allows others to be witnessed, but have their own experience, and therefore be able to find their own power and resilience.

Shine bright

Spread your full wing span and take up space. It's exhausting trying to be someone you're not. Stop that. Do you, boo. The right ones can find you easier when you shine!

Accept Compliments

When someone pays you a compliment try saying, "Thank you..." with no further response.

It can be excruciatingly painful at first to actually allow a genuine compliment in (side note: genuine compliments have nothing to do with what we do or have, they are reflections back about our character, our inner beauty, our expression of self and love and kindness in the world). But sister, I know you want to live in a world of JOY, PEACE, LOVE, ABUNDANCE and HARMONY, so that means you gotta let the good shit in! And OWN it!

Own your outrageous sense of humor, your sharp wit or intellect, own your beautiful curves, your strength and your softness. Own your stretchmarks too, my how you have grown into the brilliant being you are now! Own your deep sexual drive and desire, hell, own the fact that you're GOOD AT SEX! Own your incredible artistic skills and the way you move mountains with your words. Own your big dreams and the way you LIVE them! Own your quirks and idiosyncrasies. Own your curiosity and the way you challenge the status quo.

OWN IT ALL. Do not back down, do not dim your light, do not shrink in other people's fear. And by all means, do NOT apologize for any of it.

Queens create their own standard of success

Part of not apologizing for yourself is about learning to let go of society's standards of success. Maybe getting a PhD or becoming CEO is success to you. Maybe success looks like letting go of the 9-5 grind and finally allowing yourself to acknowledge that all you've ever really wanted to do was be a stay at home mom and teach your kids how to grow their own food. Neither option, or anything in between is right or wrong. Neither one is more successful. True women's liberation is about the power to choose.

We practice sacrament 1 so we can slow down long enough to hear what's actually true for us. We Practice Sacrament 2 to acknowledge how that truth feels in our body. We practice Sacrament 3 to fortify our right to embody that Truth. Like Joan of Arc, we move unapologetically in the direction of that Truth, and in a world that doesn't want us to do that we become textbook-level history makers. If you're moving in the direction of what is most honest for you, and no one else, then please consider yourself WILDLY SUCCESSFUL.

Own it, don't owe it

Guilt vs. Shame

Guilt says "I've done something wrong," shame says "I am wrong." When a woman is constantly apologizing for herself, overtly or covertly, she creates a neural pathway of shame. This shame becomes a baseline existence, like a sticky residue that's always there. So even when good things come in, such as a genuine compliment or an award, she can't receive it, there's nowhere in her cells to actually take it in. So she deflects, she self-deprecates, or just flat out rejects the praise.

This constant rejection signals to the Universe that positive energy or experiences are unwelcomed, so slowly but surely, they stop arriving. When the compliments, achievements, blessings and gifts start disappearing, it weaves a narrative of lack in a woman's life. Real scarcity begins to set in, and it can often become a self-fulfilling prophecy.

Our apologies can in effect bankrupt us. Or even cause dis-ease or illness. As Lynne Twist says, "What you appreciate, appreciates."

Your lack of apology will inspire a revolution of genuine happiness. Because every moment when you could choose to apologize for something, but instead choose to acknowledge it or own it, you are exercising positive choice. Happiness isn't a single place in heaven we reach when we've magically made everyone else around us comfortable and content. Happiness is a state of being felt and expressed with literally

every

Single

Positive

Choice

We

Make

In the direction of

Happiness

Critical Thinking Skills

As good little girls, we've been programmed to perform compliance. We're considered "good" if we comply with our family system, our educational system, our medical or government systems.

First I ask you, how does that feel? How does the frequency of compliance feel in your body, your heart, your Soul?

Next, I invite you to consider how change happens in the world and notice whether change has ever been created by someone who was compliant. Your critical thinking skills are the bridge to your capacity to make change in your life, or perhaps even the world. Your thoughts, opinions, ideas and inspirations are a threat to others who fear change, but conversely they will be pure medicine to those who are ready for the sacred rebellion required for a life beyond the status quo.

Say it with me, "**I AM NO LONGER WILLING TO APOLOGIZE FOR**..." scream, write in your journal, do a dance, whatever floats your boat, but whatever you do, declare your relationship to unnecessary apologies complete here and now across all times and space.

That way, when there is actually something for you to apologize for, the apology is filled with so much integrity and clarity that it can't help but create full on alchemy. You will actually begin to honor the act of apology because it will be filled with genuine self-responsibility, no guilt, no shame whatsoever.

Personal Story:

The impossible is made possible when we unapologetically stand in our Truth.

I never intended to fall in love with women. It just kind of happened.

There are parts of my journey where I understand my sexuality to be somewhat of a trauma response to an abusive relationship with a man in my early 20's. When I really feel for what's true, though, I make contact with the part of me that simply shows up for Love. The one in me who knows that it's not about the form, it's about the energy, the soul contract, the karma, the whatever you want to call it, which frankly, can also just be "Hey, you're really fucking hot!"

In my early 20's, I fell in love with Jen. In my mid-20's I fell in love with Liz. I didn't pursue same-sex love, it found me, and who was I to shut the door on love? It is my queer journey that has alway brought me back to Sacrament 3. Queer in my experience of sexual fluidity, but also queer in the larger non-conforming sense. I didn't come here to be normal, I came here to be me. I came here to be honest, birthmarks and all.

My entire queer journey was spent on the West Coast of California and Chilean Patagonia, where I spent a year teaching English in the backdrop of National Geographic.

"Don't tell the business," was a famous family line, and one that particularly rubbed me the wrong way, but during my exploration of sexuality it actually provided me a freedom, a maintaining of boundaries when I needed them the most. Thousands of miles away, no one could judge me for that which I wasn't ready to be judged for.

The first person I came out to was my father. I waited until I had broken up with Jen to tell him I'd been in love with a woman for the last year of my life. I also told him that my knees equally buckled when I saw a gorgeous man walk down the street. There was no difference for me. I told my dad this over BBQ, cornbread, and beers, like ya do when you're raised in the South, and I'll never forget the expression on my dad's face when he heard this news. His eyes widened with surprise, he took a breath, a swig of beer for good measure, and then uttered the words I needed to hear, "Whatever makes you happy, Sarah. I must say, I'm a bit surprised, but I love you, and I will always support you. Please do whatever makes you happy."

This first step is what made all the other steps possible. When we stop hiding in one facet of our lives, we begin to fortify our capacity for unapologetic radiance in all areas of our lives; a gradual coming-out, regardless of sexuality.

Jen had come and gone, a few men following her found their way into my heart-womb space, but by and large the next love of my life was Liz. This felt different, it was deeper, less experimental, more real.

Like maybe I was really going to do this as my life partnership framework? Six months went by, and I felt strongly that Liz was going to be in my life for a long time. My relationship with her also intersected with my growth and expansion of being in grad school; I was learning how to not apologize at an exponential rate, so holding things in no longer fit my moral compass.

As someone who grew up very close to my grandparents, talking every week, it was becoming harder and harder to hide why I was so darn happy with my life in San Francisco. This was particularly hard to hide from my Granny, because she was my best friend from the day I was born. How do you keep such a good thing from your BFF? Even if it was she who coined "Don't tell the business."

I distinctly remember walking to my favorite neighborhood cafe, sitting in the window, nestled behind rows of tables, and dialing my grandmother's number. "Oh Sarah, love! How are you? It's so good to hear from you. What's doing in San Francisco this week?"

"Hi Granny, um, do you have a moment? I want to share something with you."

"Of course, Love Bug, what's up?"

In that moment, I felt my solar plexus begin to churn. I wanted to puke, but also knew I needed to share this. It was hard to breathe, but I did my damndest to stay present in the moment.

My Granny, part spit-fire, part Mother Mary, loved me more than anything in the world, but was also deeply Catholic. Was I about to lose my best friend?

Like being pushed off the diving board before you're fully ready for that backflip, the words just started to vomit, "Granny, well, I need to tell you that I've been seeing someone for the last six months."

"Oh really? Do tell!"

"Well, they're absolutely amazing, and I feel so, so happy, but I need to tell you, it's a woman. I'm in love with a woman. Her name is Liz. We met through mutual friends. Granny?"

"Oh my," she chuckled, "let me get my cigarettes..." Once she had done that, she said, "Okay," took a puff, then told me, "Ok Lovey, well, I love you, and I always will, and if this is what makes you happy then this makes my heart happy. She better be good to you, you hear? And if there's any funny business you just let me know. You deserve the best."

Fucking. Floored.

My Irish Catholic grandmother simply needed a puff of a cigarette and one deep breath to know and honor and accept that what we were talking about was LOVE. And that it was because of her profound Love for me, she could see past religious ideologies about constructs of Love, and instead support the frequency of Love I was blessed to give and receive. I showed up, unapologetically, to own my Truth to a person I loved, shaking in my boots, but knowing the choice of no-choice. In turn, the seemingly impossible was made possible.

In fact, all is made possible through Love, and it is the radical Love of Self that empowers us to stand tall in the Truth of who we are, knowing that this full expression of Self is the most sacred permission slip we could give others. When we are given full permission to Love and be Loved, separation begins to dissolve, and in its place grows a unity that brings healing to our bodies, all our relations, and to the very Earth we walk on.

Own it, don't owe it, and I guarantee you will move generational mountains in the name of Love.

P.S. Do you think for a second Mary Magdalene apologized or dimmed her light for Jesus? Hell no! It was her light which was the very point of attraction that made their Union possible in the first place. It was her full fledged radiance that commanded respect from Him. It was Her light that anointed and emboldened Him to rise into the man He fully became. A Love like that is terrifying to systems and structures that benefit from your fear, but a Love like that always comes out on top, even if it's 2,000 years later.

Trust in your capacity to lean into the fire, so that anything standing in the way of you fully fucking shining can be burned. Anything standing in the way of Love can leave.

Practicing Sacrament 3
Overview

Shadow: Arrogance, attention-seeking behavior, narcissism, insensitivity to others, use of manipulation or coercion to get needs met.

Chakra: This Sacrament is connected to the 3rd Chakra, located at your solar plexus. This chakra radiates a vibrant yellow or golden frequency. This chakra is connected to your sense of will, personal power, authority and autonomy, capacity to shine your light in the world, sense of self-esteem and self-confidence, make decisions, and take action. This chakra is connected to your digestion and metabolism, not just of food but also of energy, so it can be a great chakra to work with in relation to your energetic boundaries.

We begin feeling for our boundaries in Sacrament/Chakra 2, but we assert them or define them in Sacrament/Chakra 3. Working with this chakra can support the release of poor self-discipline, discernment, and victim mentality, so as to step into greater personal power and responsibility.

Earth Cycles

Moon phases: This Sacrament is Full Moon ALL THE WAY! I love standing outside on a Full Moon, naked if weather permits, and unapologetically howling as loudly as possible! Other ways to unapologetically work with the lunar cycles is to take each Full Moon to celebrate something about yourself you love. Blast a selfie or your message out on social media, call a good friend to brag in a healthy way, or ask to be witnessed by friends, family or a larger audience in a skill or gift of yours (hello open mic night!). The Full Moon is an energy of amplification, so practicing NO APOLOGIES under this lunation will amplify your intentions for strong self-confidence and shining brightly throughout the lunar cycle, and frankly, all the time!

Seasons: This Sacrament is Summer, baby! Think full radiant summer sunshine! Even in the dead of Winter, we can bring Summer to ourselves and the world around us when we unapologetically shine our light. This can be in subtle or large ways; always trust that you know how to BE in the essence of this Sacrament. Perhaps it's a color you're wearing, a bright meal you prepare, a bouquet of fresh cut flowers you adorn your kitchen table with, or smiling brightly at a random stranger on the street. You'll know you're aligning with this Sacrament and the Seasonal benefits of Summer by the amount of *Joy* you feel and are willing to give and receive from the world. Be the Summer in someone else's Winter and I guarantee the miraculous will follow you! Shit, be the Summer in your own Winter and no doubt your world will change for the better.

Supports

Mantras:

- I call all of my power back to me here and now!
- No is a complete sentence.
- Return to sender (when returning energy to a person or situation that doesn't belong to you).
- My light lights up the world!
- When I shine bright, it gives others permission to do the same.
- I am not too much.
- I will not shrink myself to make others feel more comfortable.
- I am radiance.
- I am allowed to take up space.
- I release outsourcing and return to in-sourcing (my own power, pleasure, truth, expression, etc.)
- My full self is welcome here.
- I am powerful.

Divine Feminine allies:

- Kali
- Sekhmet
- Sheela-Na-Gig

Herbal ally: Wood Betony

- *The* solar plexus herb. A taste of wood betony releases tension and summons fire. She helps us to stand strongly and unapologetically in who we are, what we're here to do, and how we're doing it. Period.

- This herb can be ingested through teas, tinctures, flower essences, infused honey and elixirs. It can also be topically applied in hydrosol mists or body sprays. However, simply meditating on this herb can bring powerful insight and awareness.

Songs:

- "The Power" by SNAP!
- "Power" by Goapele
- "Unharnessed" by The Human Experience, Leah Song
- "Woman" by Diana Gordon
- "Authors of Forever" by Alicia Keys
- " La Medicina" by Suculima
- "Trollabundin" by Eivor
- "Bowls" by Caribou
- "I See God in You" by India Arie
- "Soy Yo" by Bomba Estereo
- "Golden" by Jill Scott
- "This is Me" by Keala Settle, The Greatest Showman Ensemble
- " Show Yourself" by Aylah Nereo

Integration tools:

Honesty. When someone asks "how are you?" answer honestly (not just "I'm fine.") If this is new for you, practice responding this way to someone you know will hold a loving, non judgemental space for your answer AND someone who won't immediately jump into fixing or problem solving if your answer is one filled with struggle or complexity.

Brag. (i.e. celebrate your wins, accomplishments, talents, beauty, manifestations)

Reject ill-fitting labels. When someone asks you what you do for a living, answer them in a way that feels good to YOU, don't try to package it in digestible words that make it easier for others to understand. Instead, invite people into a dialogue about what you do, create a bridge for them to learn something new. I explain what a doula is A LOT, as mainstream still isn't quite on board with bringing this ancient role back into modern day birthwork. The 7 Sacraments of the Goddess is always an interesting conversation starter, too!

Adorn authentically. Wear clothing that makes YOU feel good and reflects your true essence (part of Sacrament 2, as well).

Invest in yourself. Spend money on things that support you achieving your dreams, healing, being nourished, making an impact, and shining!

Acknowledge & appreciate, don't apologize. Unless there is something to genuinely apologize for, practice simply acknowledging the feelings of others and expressing gratitude for their grace.

Dance in public. I do this A LOT!!! When I lived in cities, I used to dance on public transit, but nowadays I dance on the beach. It never fails to inspire people to come up to me and begin a conversation about JOY!

Wear gold or yellow. Invite these colors into your life in playful ways (food, home decor, fashion, your website or social media).

Honor your desire. Spend a whole day doing whatever YOU want, and let your body guide you every step of the way (I suggest doing this once a month so your system gets used to feeling as a gift you give yourself for authentic self-care and NOT something to feel guilty about). My favorite is getting dressed up and taking myself on dates. Bring a book, a journal, or just myself, order a really good glass of wine, and people-watch. Fully experiencing my own energy this way actually opens me up to experiencing the world around me more fully than if I was focused on someone else on that date. I've never not had a miracle or synchronistic run-in with someone while dating myself!

Invocations

Prayer:

Divine Mother, I pray to give zero fucks! I pray for Your assistance in helping me release any tendrils of fear, doubt, or shame that would get in the way of that. Through Your unconditional Love and protection, I pray to call all my power back to me across all times, spaces, dimensions, and Universes, so that my fullest Self can be, here, NOW.

Divine Mother, help me to shine brightly in the world, and may my unapologetic shining give others full permission to do the same. May my life be a walking prayer of radiant self-worth and self-commitment, and may the luminous offering of my life bring healing to all women who came before and all women who will come after.

I pray to be a Lighthouse for myself, others, and the Earth Herself. And if I lose my way, I call on you, dear Goddess, and allow your grace to fortify my capacity for Queendom here on Earth. Every breath, every moment, of every day. And so it is.

Journal prompts

Self, Relationships, Earth

Sarah Grady, MA

Homecoming

Maiden, Mother, Crone

Free write

Elemental release and reclaim ceremony

This Sacrament is purely connected to the element of Fire. As such I encourage women to work with the fire of their personal radiance, as well as the fire of anger and rage. As women we've been told that our anger is wrong, and this couldn't be further from the truth.

So, you'll find a ritual below to honor your sacred rage, as well as your sacred radiance. We need not apologize for either in this lifetime, for they are equally important expressions and personal medicine.

Radiant Burn: gather a journal, candle or fire, and something golden (e.g., a piece of jewelry or yellow food).

Light your candle or fire, and just as we've done in the first 2 Sacraments, write down or speak to the fire any and all ways in which you are releasing the frequency of apologizing from your life. This can include limiting beliefs and imprints passed down to you from family, society, educational or political systems, media, etc. Any beliefs around what it means to be a "good girl or lady" and just let it all go.

Blow the candle out and then re-light it to speak forgiveness for any and all times you dimmed your light in any way. Forgive others who taught you that dimming your light was the only way to stay safe or get your needs met.

When you've fully forgiven, blow out the candle and take 3 deep cleansing breaths.

Let the energy settle.

Then re-light the candle one last time and verbally reclaim and call back all of your power and energy to yourself across all timelines.

Dance, strip down naked, shake your body, crawl, do whatever you're physically and emotionally guided to do in front of the fire to reclaim your full radiance. Maybe you speak a prayer to the fire for support and helping you to shine brightly in new areas of your life. Maybe you call-in a particular ally or guide to walk with you on the journey of

No Apologies. Trust whatever comes through and when you feel like you've fully declared this reclamation to the fire complete your ritual by saying "I am allowed to take up space. I am allowed to shine brightly. I am worthy of being fully me!"

And so it is.

Blow out your candle and adorn yourself with your radiant jewelry or eat your golden honey, pineapple or any other item you've procured for this ritual.

Sacred rage ceremony: Your anger and rage are not to be repressed, sister, they are sacred messengers here with information related to your deepest healing and evolution This ritual gives them the proper space to do so.

You can make this as simple or as elaborate as you want to. When I'm feeling rage, I know I need to channel that energy physically, so I always gather a good pillow, make a playlist full of strong drumbeats or guttural throat singing, make sure I have lots of water, a journal close by for integration afterwards, and a friend to witness (although this can certainly be done by yourself if you prefer.) I light a candle, I invoke sacred space by asking my spirit guides and higher self to be present, I say a prayer that my rage be alchemized into whatever information or healing I need, then I press play on playlist and LET IT RIP! By which I mean, start punching the shit out of your pillow, couch, bed or all of it! In fact, I love using a pillow to smack a couch or bed, it's like a middle school pillow fight but way better!

It might start sort of slow or even awkward, but I guarantee you'll catch a rhythm and eventually all that angry energy inside of you will know how to move and discharge.

You'll keep punching your pillow until you physically feel a completion come on.

Turn the music off and just sit in silence for a moment. Feel how your body feels, take a few deep cleansing breaths to ground, and then notice your emotional body. What thoughts or feels are coming up? Any insights or divine messages coming through? Write them down or record them in a voice memo on your phone.

If a friend was present with you during this ritual ask if they have any words of reflection or support for you, or simply a hug can be quite healing during a moment like this.

Blow out your candle and give thanks to yourself, your sacred space, to any energetic guides that showed up spiritually to support your process, and of course, to your sacred rage...thank her for visiting, thank her for her wisdom, thank her for the opportunity to know your aliveness through the frequency of her.

Your ritual is now complete.

Sacrament 4:

Heart Compass

Re-membering

There was a time when people prayed from the heart, spoke from the heart, moved from the heart and lived from the heart.

There was a time when grief was seen as just as sacred as joy, and love was a healing technology, not an image on a movie screen.

There was a time when no words needed to be spoken, because all was felt through the unified field of the heart; we could touch each other from continents away.

There was a time when we loved each other because we knew what Love meant.

This time wasn't without challenge, but it was simpler, and more courageous.

Remember this time.

Heart Compass

"Love liberates."

— Maya Angelou

If you've been bold enough to introduce Sacraments 1-3 into your life, you may notice a snowglobe-like effect; shit is getting shaken up and you're wondering how the hell all the little particles will settle and find their way home again.

This, my love, is where the wise guidance of your heart comes in. It's your loving steering wheel to grab onto when you're in need of guided action and have no idea where to start. The heart compass, just like a mechanical compass, has four cardinal directions (see diagram in the next section). The difference, however, is the reciprocal nature of the heart compass *energetically*. In other words, the electrical frequencies given out by the heart also garner frequencies returned; you're not just going north to go north. What you give out, even to yourself, will be returned to you; it is law. The form may surprise you, but to be sure, it always returns.

In the realm of feminine embodiment, it's important to be clear that there is both the high heart, and the low heart. The high heart is in your physical heart, while the low heart is your womb space. Both spaces carry deep intelligence within a woman's body and being. Even when specific organs have been removed, there is still an energetic imprint of wisdom operating in the system. When a woman consciously dialogues with both hearts, and invites them to work in synergy, she then has access to her full central channel. In short, she has full access to the core of who she is.

We all know the difference between making a decision from a place of "I should do this…" rather than "this feels right." The heart will always invite you into your expansion through sensation or feeling. The ego will try to keep you safe and comfortable, which often maintains a state of contraction. When we can feel into our heart's truth and then get our brain power behind that truth, for practical or logistical reasons, we tend to take aligned action that not only works in our favor but fills us with a deep sense of integrity and pride.

This sense of personal alignment is contrary to the patriarchal narrative that to follow one's heart is frivolous, flaky, idealistic, irresponsible, ungrounded, or flat-out stupid. Furthermore, our societal programming often relegates heart-led decisions to a particular period of life, such as our youth, when it's seen as acceptable to have fun and make mistakes. But when one reaches mature adulthood, more rational, practical ways of living are expected.

No my dear, to keep regular communion and communication with your heart, is actually the most rational thing you can do.

The next time you feel pulled between your head and heart, remember this fun fact: The electrical component of the heart is 60 times greater than the brain. In fact, the electromagnetic field of the heart is 5,000 times greater than the brain, and can be felt 3ft away in any direction. [1] In other words, your heart actually has far more power and sensory capacity to perceive your reality than the brain ever will. Your mind is incredibly powerful, but science proves the heart to be more so. Next time someone asks you, "Why did you do that?" with a twinge of judgment in their voice. Simply smile and answer, "Because my heart told me to."

The funny thing about the heart is that it often doesn't "make sense" in the moment. But because it is guiding us towards our expansion, we tend to see the divine hand in our heart-led actions in hindsight, often working out better than we could've anticipated. It's that classic example of following your heart's guidance to move across the country, without having ever been to where you're moving to, only to meet the love of your life in the apartment 3 doors down from where your new home is after a decade of being single.

The heart loves to dream a bigger dream for us than we would dream for ourselves. Sometimes our expansion is to lean into challenging conversations we would normally avoid, in order to know the power of speaking our Truth after years of staying silent. Other times it is to allow ourselves the audacity of receiving more love, joy, and abundance than we ever thought possible! Both instances are a homecoming because they both invite us to rise into the more of us.

When you drop into your heart and feel fear about what it is guiding you towards, take time to slow down and ask yourself if there is genuine cause for concern. If there is, heed that message and wait until a more appropriate solution arises that *feels* right.

However, there can often be a thin line between fear and excitement. Trust yourself to know the difference. Trust your heart to guide you in the right direction, be patient enough to wait for it, and call in reinforcements when you need to (see Sacrament 5.)

You are NOT crazy for following your heart. You are a bold woman reclaiming her homecoming. Our world is currently lost at sea on the waves of facts and figures, but eventually the data of the heart will become louder, and humanity will re-member its True North. Keep going.

HEART COMPASS

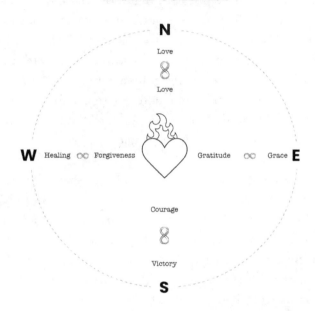

North: Love-Love

South: Courage-Victory/Success

West: Forgiveness-Healing

East: Gratitude-Grace

Note on the heart compass: Think of each direction like an infinity loop or boomerang. Love begets more Love. Courage begets Victory or Success. Forgiveness begets Healing. Gratitude begets Grace. Be open to new definitions of each quality of the heart. In other words, be willing to lift the veil of seeing what action/outcome you want so you can receive the action/outcome that is in your highest and best good.

Remember that there is no right or wrong way to approach this. Don't try to narrow things down to one direction of the heart. When approaching a decision you might be guided to start with one direction, which eventually leads you to explore one or two more in order to fully process the situation at hand. Move with curiosity and trust.

This doesn't have to take a long time, either. Sometimes all a woman needs is the permission to drop into her heart space and, as soon as she does, she just *knows* the answer she's looking for. This is why we practice Sacrament 1 first. The simple act of slowing down to create space for ourselves often accelerates the receiving of our Truth. It makes our sacred, sensual, sovereign journey energetically efficient.

Examples

Let's apply the Heart Compass to some familiar challenging relational patterns. Say you feel like the black sheep of your family, or simply have a challenging relationship with your family of origin in general. This dynamic may make the holiday season hard, for example. Past programming would say that a "good" child would participate in holiday family functions as expected, which could cause personal anxiety at the least, or a re-traumatization at most. Either outcome is potentially avoidable by tuning into the heart compass for clear, loving, sovereign guidance about how to navigate the holidays in a more generative way instead.

North: Love.

The frequency of Love might lead you to create a time container on your family holiday time. In other words, you set a boundary of spending one night or one meal with your family instead of a full week. This feels loving to yourself to create a boundary that supports your nervous system, while also signaling to your family that you care about spending time with them. OR What feels most loving might actually be skipping the holidays with family altogether and asking them to schedule a different time of year to spend quality time together when there's less stress and pressure.

South: Courage.

It takes courage to set boundaries with family as adult children. These boundaries might trigger intense responses from family members who feel confused or rejected by your personal choices. However, the victory/success gained from courageously asserting this boundary could be two-fold: 1) You feel a sense of self-love and pride knowing you're doing what's best for you, and 2) Your family may begin to start honoring you as a sovereign adult, not just the child they want to keep in a familiar role for their comfort. This could ultimately lead to a much healthier relationship in the long run.

West: Forgiveness.

In this process of boundary setting during the holidays you may directly, or indirectly through prayer, ceremony, ritual, or personal healing session forgive your family members for any past pain they may have caused you. In turn you may receive a sense of personal healing and relief, but you may also explicitly notice a shift in your family dynamics. Those shifts might be subtle or large, and they could unfold in an unusual timeline (e.g. it might be six months after you've said the prayer or done the ritual that a shift in relationship

142

occurs), but to be sure, you'll notice a tendril of healing somewhere in your process simply because you decided to move out of resentment and into forgiveness. Our clear and pure intentions always have a positive ripple effect.

East: Gratitude.

By first courageously creating loving boundaries, and then dropping into the frequency of forgiveness, we can then come to a place of genuine gratitude for who our family is, instead of who they are not. For example, your mother might not know how to meet you emotionally, but she might be really good at throwing parties and gathering people for moments of light-hearted celebration. During the holidays, you can praise her for being someone who creates beauty, joy and connection through celebration. In expressing gratitude, directly or indirectly to her about these qualities, this liberates her to be more of that which you love, and it liberates you from needing her to be anything else in those moments. This liberation creates space for grace. Grace might be a loving time with her that you didn't think was possible before. Grace might be the experience of feeling deeply mothered by someone you're not biologically related to at the holidays instead.

Love lets go.

The frequency of Love does not grasp, cling, control, defend, push, or try to be "right." True Love lets go.

Love steps aside with the understanding that a greater intelligence is orchestrating everything, and that [that] intelligence is benevolent.

True love lets people go if they are not ready to meet us on the bridge of relationship.

True Love allows others to make "mistakes" so they may find their own power and integrity.

True Love softens where before we may have hardened for self-protection.

In the moments when it feels like Love is coming in fiercely it's often to guide us South into the direction of our Courage. Courage is a love emboldened with purpose without being righteous. It is one of the most active ways we can embody love. But no matter what form it comes in, Love lets go because it has no agenda other than Love.

When in doubt ask, "What would Love do?"

Mind vs. Heart

The mind can rationalize anything. The Heart will tell you the Truth.

That Truth may be inconvenient, humbling or hard to hear, but you will know it as Truth because of the feeling it brings your body; Truth brings you deeper IN. As such, we start by going into our hearts so that we can touch the heart of any matter that ails us.

The Truth of the heart will keep knocking on your door until you answer. You always have free will to choose whether to listen or not, but the heart will get louder and louder until it feels like you don't. Be brave enough to listen to the whispers before they become sirens.

Sacred Union

The physical heart is the meeting place in the body of the above and the below. Every wisdom tradition has a different language for this: Father Sky and Mother Earth, Masculine and Feminine, Heaven and Earth, or Hanan Pacha and Kay Pacha.

More broadly speaking, our heart is the alchemical center of opposites. All the seemingly opposing forces of shadow and light that exist within us can be transformed through the power of the heart. When we regularly sit with our heart, as we would a trusted counselor, we begin to soften our split ways of perceiving the world and instead come into a more compassionate, holistic schema. The heart can hold the paradoxical nature of life.

Ever been upset with someone but still deeply love them at the same time? People want to be around other people rooted in their heart because they sense there will be more love and less judgment when in their presence. Imagine, then, how good it would feel to be in your own company from this place. Imagine that it might feel like home.

To be rooted in the heart is the true sacred marriage we're all after, not the wedding fanfare on social media. As such, when you feel like someone or something is missing, including a part of yourself, take time to sit with your heart. This might look like physically holding it, tapping on it, dialoguing with it and journaling your responses, or playing music that fills your heart with energy. Trust what you're guided to do, and go slow enough to hear the messages of your heart speak to you in this space. It will give you clues about the true purpose of your longing.

Grief work

In the West, we live in a grief-phobic culture. There is no proper container for our grief and we're often told to put a specific time limit on it.

For example, there's a death in the family, you're allowed to go to the funeral and cry for a week and then magically somehow you're expected to return to "normal" shortly thereafter. You lose your job and are immediately expected to jump right into job searching. You suffer a break-up and are told to get back in the dating pool again, as if a new person automatically erases the loss of another. "Toughen up, grow thicker skin, buck up, get on with it, etc." These tend to be patriarchal mantras inserted into our psyches to make others feel more comfortable about our discomfort.

Well, grief doesn't work that way. The heart doesn't work that way. The Feminine sure as shit doesn't work that way. And news flash, most other cultures around the world don't work that way, either. Most indigenous cultures actively grieve on a regular basis as part of routine mental and spiritual healthcare. Imagine what would happen to the pharmaceutical industry if we gave ourselves the gift of grief.

The feminine does not care about your desired timeline, she cares about your authenticity, your growth, and your healing. Maybe you'll experience loss and you truly will feel resolution after one week of actively grieving. Maybe the same grief will keep arising for ten years straight because there's a deeply embedded lesson you must learn or a part of yourself to be reclaimed.

The old saying is, "the only way out is through," and if this is true, the Feminine invites us into the portal of the heart compass so we can release our shame and make it through our grief with as much love, courage, forgiveness and gratitude as possible. To grieve something is to acknowledge your love for it. Allowing ourselves the wild gift of grief ultimately fortifies our capacity for greater Love.

In this way, grief, too, is a homecoming, to the totality of who we really are, and how much we are capable of Loving. Know, then, that your grief is always pointing you towards True North on your compass. To grieve is to actively let Love lead. When this way of loving feels inconvenient or challenges your other relationships, be sure to remember Sacrament 3: No Apologies. Your grief is not necessarily something for you or others to understand. It is more an alchemical process of transformation led by Love into more Love. The best you can do is allow it.

Re-parenting oneself

When we get triggered as adults, it's often because it touches on an unresolved wound from our childhoods. Even if we have great relationships with our parents, at some point in our development, it's natural and important to step into our own internal parent role. The heart is the access point for this re-parenting.

Homecoming

In the sad or scary moments of childhood, all we wanted was a parent to love and comfort us. This is no different in adulthood. It is empowering to know that through accessing the wisdom of the heart we can listen for how to give ourselves that love and comfort. The heart may guide you to fulfill the need for love with self-soothing or it may invite you to receive support from a trusted friend, partner or healing practitioner.

The most direct way I know how to re-parent myself is to physically hold my heart, like I would a baby's bottom, rock it back and forth and simply ask the little one in me "what do you need?" Keep asking that question until you feel like you've hit the core answer. It may be as simple as needing a hug or someone to affirm you're doing a great fucking job at life. It may be that you need more play and creativity to lighten up all the work and stress in your life. It may be that you need to have really hot, rough sex and get in touch with a primal part of yourself you let go of when you were young. Don't judge what answer you get, just focus on doing your best to meet that need.

Over time you'll be amazed at how good it feels to meet your own needs. You'll also become much less resentful of your own parents for not being able to meet them in childhood, or even now in adulthood. They, too, are flawed human beings like the rest of us doing the best they can with what they know. Allow yourself to know more than them if that's what's required for your healing. Your lineage will thank you.

The impossible becomes possible through Love.

Repeat after me: "Because I want to, is just as good a reason as any."

The heart wants what it wants. Stop trying to create a justifiable reason why you're allowed to follow it. You'll sleep better at night if you follow the heart-knowing inside you. It might take you six years to get up the courage to take action on that wanting whisper, but that's ok, you're not on anyone's timeline except your own. It's never too late.

---

1. Heart Math Institute, www.heartmath.org

Personal Story:

When we choose to follow our heart compass, our giving is always met with reciprocity. We remember our receiving as holy.

A month after I quit my psychotherapy job, I hopped on a plane to Costa Rica for level 2 of Qoya Teacher Training. Quit job, get the fuck out of dodge, I think it's a healthy equation for life!

I had no idea what was in store for me in the jungle, I just knew I needed to go. My body told me, and I was obedient. I'm so glad I listened.

For seven days I danced, cried, swam in the ocean, burned through layers of fear I didn't even know were there. I deeply bonded with other sisters, and was initiated into the next level of Qoya as my way of life; this is not just a movement practice, it is a practice that moves you from a place of deep physical sensations of Truth. Qoya does translate to Queen, in Quechua, after all. And per Sacrament 1, we know that Sovereignty can only be built upon Truth. Qoya teaches us how to do that from a divinely feminine, embodied place. We don't think our way into Sovereignty, we feel it.

I decided to spend a few extra days after the training by myself in the sweet surf town of Nosara. This little town is no joke. It is for sure a portal in its own right. I felt a distinctly Divine Feminine presence there, and found myself addressing Nosara as She, as if She were a person.

Ever notice how your heart guides you to different places on Earth and you immediately feel a relationship? Sometimes I feel a sense of home, other times I equate a new city to a lover. There's a sensation of kindred that creates safety, and in this safety we let the walls of our heart down to allow ourselves to be led by Love.

One afternoon in Nosara, I happened upon the Bazaar Boutique. I'd heard about this place from several of the women in my teacher training. It was the infamous shop where many of them had procured gorgeous goddess dresses for our evening ceremonies. I didn't have money to spend, I didn't even have a job to return to when I landed back in the Bay, so I sheepishly made my way around the store as a silent observer.

That lasted for all of 5 seconds before Kelly, the shop clerk who'd relocated from New Jersey, struck up a conversation with me. One thing led to the next, and I revealed that I was engaged to be married. Naturally, she asked if I had a dress, and I declared that I hadn't yet found the right one. As fate would have it, Kelly had recovered a white dress earlier in the day that had fallen between one of the clothing racks. The only one of its kind in the store. She insisted that I try it on. I was hot and sweaty, carrying a coconut. This was NOT my wedding dress shopping moment. Still, she insisted.

Homecoming

As I put my things down, I heard a voice whisper from deep within, "Just try it on, you never know!"

Holy of holies! I slid this dress on—made from one long piece of fabric, with a single seam up the back—and it literally fit like a second skin. The body of the dress meets the seam of a train that can literally be wrapped around the body in 15 different ways. The only decor on the whole dress were tiny red beads and shells sewn onto the very end of the train. At one point, Kelly took the fabric and draped it over my head. Like the red-hooded priestess Mary Magdalene, or the goddess Isis, I stood in the mirror trying in vain to catch my breath, unsure of which timeline I was standing in.

This wasn't just my wedding dress, it was my sacred skin.

I came back to Earth and, in a breath, began to panic about how much it cost and the fact that I hadn't eaten in hours. I asked Kelly for lunch spot suggestions, and sheepishly asked her to hold the dress for me so I could make a decision from a more grounded and nourished place. She winked at me, slid the dress behind the counter, and directed me to *the* place I must go to for lunch.

If you've been to Nosara, you know the main street is not big, it's really hard to miss something, so when I couldn't find this one fucking lunch spot, I became a bit exasperated. After several laps around town, I was stopped by a loud voice, full of laughter. I looked up, and there was the restaurant that had been evading me this whole time. I made a b-line for the counter and ordered, but I had to pass the tall, loud, laughing American man on my way to the counter. I was somewhat embarrassed and intrigued when he gestured for me to come sit with him and his companion. Initially, I declined, but as I finished my meal in sacred solitude, that physical sensation of Truth started to creep up. "Go sit with him," it whispered. Sometimes my heart guidance is really annoying and inconvenient. But again, I'm obedient, and 9 times out of 10, I'm grateful that I listened.

I pulled up a chair next to "Beach," and his companion, also named Sarah. Two ex-pats trying to find their Truth in the middle of Costa Rica. Beach came here to heal his body after burnout in corporate, and Sarah left a husband and high paying job at Tiffany's in the UK to be a wedding cake maker, of all things. From the start it was one of those cosmic conversations where I wondered how many lifetimes we'd all known each other. I could tell we were contracted to midwife something together, I just didn't know it was they who had agreed to midwife me.

As conversation flowed, Sarah commented on my ring, and I told her it was my engagement ring. Immediately, Beach said, "Oh, tell us about the lucky guy," to which I replied with my journey of falling in love with a woman, and coming to the understanding of my sexuality as fluid.

The expression on Beach's face sank. He began to well with tears, and then proceeded to profusely apologize. Not so coincidentally, he'd just had a conversation with his very conservative brother back in Ohio, discussing LGBTQ rights and relationships, and it didn't go very well. There was something about the intersection of our lives in that moment that sparked an inner declaration for Beach: Love is love is love. Period.

The next natural place the conversation went was whether I had a dress or not, to which I almost spit out my coconut water as I told them about my encounter at Bazaar Boutique just one hour prior.

Sarah and Beach both declared, "This is your dress! You have to go back and get it!" But I was too hung up on the money piece. I was broke and had no business even being in Costa Rica, let alone putting another $300 on my credit card. This did not derail them. "Get the dress, you must!" They demanded. I told them I'd consider it. They invited me to a beach bonfire gathering happening later that evening, and we parted ways.

I slowly began my walk through town, thanking the Goddess that Bazaar Boutique was literally at the very end of the road. I was buying time. Every 30 minutes or so, Beach would find me in a store or walking on the street and he'd just casually ask "Are you gonna get the dress?" After the third time I was both annoyed, feeling pressured, and also deeply curious about what was really going on here. So, I decided to practice the Sacraments and slow the fuck down.

I found a random path off the main road. It was completely encapsulated by trees and tropical flowers. It felt like a place out of time. So I closed my eyes, began to breathe, and called on all my higher guidance. I held my heart with my hands as I did this. Every time I asked my heart and my body if this was my dress, I would nearly fall over. My whole body would propel forward as a resounding yes. This wasn't practical or logical, it didn't make sense, but without even knowing the directions of the heart compass yet I heard a voice whisper, "Move with courage, you cannot go wrong."

I gingerly emerged from the jungle path back to the main road and eventually back to the boutique. Without a word, Kelly smiled at me and brought the dress out from behind the counter. I asked to try it on one more time just to be sure, and as I did, Kelly motioned the shop owner and designer of the dress to come over.

The next thing I know, I'm like a model out of Vogue, being photographed and styled every which way. My whole heart knew this dress was mine, for reasons even beyond getting married to Rachel.

I looked at Kelly and said "OK, let's do it! Here's my credit card. I have no idea how I'll pay it off, but I just have to have it."

To my shock, she politely declined my card and whispered, "It's been taken care of."

"What? What do you mean it's been taken care of?"

"Well, you know that gentleman you met at lunch about an hour ago?"

That's when I stopped being able to hear the words coming out of her mouth. The tears wouldn't stop flowing from my eyes, the hairs stood up on my skin. I was shaking.

What?? A random stranger just gifted me my wedding dress?!

I eventually heard Kelly say, "He just felt really strongly that he wanted to honor your love in the world. That love is love is love, whether gay, straight or anything in between, and he wanted you to know that."

In my courage to trust that I was worthy of giving myself something, I received the victory of knowing that love would always win. I received not just a dress, but a healing that day. I received the remembering of just how held and supported by the universe I was and always would be. All that is ever required of me is to take guided action from my heart. And when I do, I will be met in that place, always.

I met Beach and Sarah on the beach later that evening, and gifted Beach a rose quartz crystal from our last day of Qoya training. I told him that imbued in this crystal was my prayer for Love. That he might know love for himself and with a beloved the way I have come to know.

I am still in touch with this man, all these years later, still rooting for his love and mine.

Although Liz and I never got married, I've worn this dress too many times to count now. Every time I facilitate a sacred ceremony, class or event, I wear this dress. Anytime I have a photo shoot for my work in the world, I wear this dress. As I stood on the Earth of Newgrange and the Hill of Tara in Ireland, I wore this dress, marrying myself, vowing to my ancestral land I would always follow my heart and shine as brightly as I could.

My ego mind would've closed me off from the miracle of this moment, but my heart kept me open. She followed her True North of Love and received more Love. She allowed me to be led by courage, and in turn I received an abundant victory. I spoke so much gratitude every step of the way, and in turn received the grace of this gift that has literally kept on giving.

And I also forgave myself for every time I didn't listen to the whispers of my heart in exchange for a more practical "smart woman" choice. In this forgiveness, I've received deep healing of ancestral wounds of scarcity. I now know that my heart will always guide me towards the abundance of the universe. The Magdalene in me knows the abundance of Love in all four directions of my heart and in the world. If I ever forget, I just put this dress on and re-member. I'm always sure to have the train fabric gracing my head, priestess hood metamorphosing into Queen crown as I anoint myself again and again.

Practicing Sacrament 4
Overview

Shadow: Blindly following the heart and not applying logic; impulsivity, ungroundedness

Chakra: This Sacrament is connected to the 4th Chakra which resides at your heart or the center of your chest. This Chakra radiates a glorious green frequency. Connected to this Chakra are your hands, arms and shoulders, as they are the physical extensions of your heart. Therefore, anytime you are touching, holding, or creating something with your hands you are engaging this Sacrament and this Chakra. Breasts and lungs are also connected to this chakra.

This chakra is all about learning how to give and receive Love. When we practice this Sacrament, we remember that Love is always True North on our compass. It is loving to the self and others for us to listen to the heart and take guided action from this place. As such, the action we're taking in the world is connected and promotes greater connection with self, others and the Earth.

Earth Cycles

Moon phases: No matter what phase the moon is in, take time to work with that energy through the portal of your heart.

For example, during the New Moon, ask your heart what prayers or intentions she has for you in the upcoming cycle. What she has to say might be different from other parts of your body or mind. During the Full Moon cycle, ask your heart what she is ready to complete, fulfill, or manifest. You can also ask her how she would like to expand or open, vs. the New Moon energies when she might want to close or contract, going inward for listening instead of opening for expression.

Seasons: Each season presents a beautiful opportunity for mediation with our heart compass.

The Winter is a time of deep heart reflection and evaluation, preparing the heart for the new beginnings of Spring. In the Spring, our heart guides us in aligned ways to the new life and opportunities seeking us. In the Fall, we harvest our heart-songs and prayers, deepening our heart-meditation on gratitude, which prepares us for the dark time of Winter to evaluate what we wish to harvest in the coming year.

Taking time to meditate with your heart once per season can be a great way to make sure you're aligning with your highest heart values and intentions, consciously choosing your co-creations with life every step of the way, and course correcting when needed.

Supports

Mantras:

- My heart will always guide me home.
- My heart knows what my mind cannot.
- My heart guides me towards the highest aligned action.
- My heart is the source of all I need to know; my mind helps me put this knowing into action.
- I re-parent myself every time I drop into my heart.
- My heart reconnects me to my original parents of Mother Earth and Father Sky, Divine Mother, Divine Father. As their divine child, I am eternally loveable.
- The nature of the heart is reciprocal. I trust that what I give out always comes back to me in aligned ways.
- I am Love.
- I am Courage.
- I am Forgiveness.
- I am Gratitude.
- I allow myself to receive Love.
- I allow myself to receive Victory and Success.
- I allow myself to receive Healing.
- I allow myself to receive Grace.

Divine Feminine allies:

- Mary Magdalene
- Mother Mary
- Kuan Yin
- Eostre or Ostara

Herbal ally: Rose

- Rose, of course! Rose provides protection (thorns), so that we can safely open our heart to intimacy with ourselves, others and the Divine. An available heart hears guiding messages clearly.
- This herb can be ingested through teas, tinctures, flower essences, infused honey and elixirs. It can also be topically applied in hydrosol mists, lotions or body sprays. However, simply meditating on this herb can bring powerful insight and awareness.

Integration tools:

ROSE EVERYTHING!!! Seriously though, Rose is the great heart opener, and a flower deeply connected to the lineage of Mary Magdalene and Mother Mary. Rose essential oil, tea, kombucha, lotion, body oil, hydrosols, literally anything you can think of to ingest or apply on your body will directly connect you to the heart and OPEN it.

Ask for guidance from the 4 directions. Buy a compass (or use the one on your cell phone) and practice standing in each direction. Call on the spirit of that direction and ask for guidance. Trust whatever messages, images or sensations come through. Then journal about what you receive.

Hold the heart. Pat it like a baby's bottom. Rock back and forth, and like a baby, ask her what she needs. This simple act of holding your heart is a physical and energetic re-parenting.

Call on Father Sky and Mother Earth. Feel your heart to be the space of the holy child that they created. Feel that Truth. Feel how supported you are by the Cosmic Father and Mother, all your needs met by them.

Dance! Dance in the 4 directions of the heart (front, side, back, side) to juicy music filled with drum beats that beat to the rhythm of the heart! You can also include circling the heart in this practice.

Ask the heart. Ask your heart what she knows for you today! Ask her how she wants to move today instead of doing what you usually do, e.g. "I usually go for a five mile run in the morning but today my heart just wants to stretch and do some intuitive movement to three songs on shuffle!"

Heartful Mindfulness. Notice the moments when you feel expansion vs contraction in your life. Where you feel expanded is where your heart is leading you; contraction is usually the mind leading from a programmed place of "should."

GREEN! The heart chakra radiates the color green. Eating green foods, wearing green clothing or jewelry, or adorning your home with green accents expands your heart compass!

Nature! Get thee in Nature...your heart will guide you. Don't think too hard about it, just go, barefoot, naked or otherwise!

Buy flowers. Bringing flowers, especially roses, or other plants into your physical space brings living love into your life.

Most importantly, say loving, kind, courageous, forgiving things to yourself including the below phrases or previously listed mantras:

- I am worthy of Love
- The way I love is beautiful
- I am easy to Love.

Invocations

Prayer:

Divine Mother, I call on you to speak to me through the directions of my Heart Compass.

When I am lost, may You guide me in the right direction. Help me find my way to Love, Courage, Forgiveness and Gratitude. Help me to know the reciprocal nature of the heart, trusting that what I genuinely give will always be returned in wise and loving ways beyond my comprehension.

May my heart-guided action in the world reflect my respect of Self and others, and create greater harmony in all my relations.

Through You, Divine Mother, may I trust in the wisdom of my heart to guide me to exactly the right person, place or situation at exactly the right time.

May I invite my mind to support the manifestation of this heart guidance. My heart knows things before I consciously know them and I humbly bow to its intelligence.

A prayer for Love to be that intelligence. A prayer for Love, as Truth North on my compass, to lead me home to myself, always, again, and again, and again, with You, great Mother, by my side.

Journal prompts:

Self, Relationships, Earth

Homecoming

Maiden, Mother, Crone

Sarah Grady, MA

Free write

Elemental release and reclaim ceremony:

This Sacrament is connected to the element of Water. Oftentimes, it is said that the space of this Sacrament is the "high heart," and the space of Sacrament 2 is the "low heart." Both these spaces are deeply connected to our divinely feminine sense of intuition, emotions, and sensual perceptions of the world around us. When aligned and in balance, both our high heart, and the lower heart of the womb, can support us flowing with the current of life instead of forcing life from a more mental or masculine place.

Please gather a vessel of water, a journal, and something to write with, as well as a candle for invocation of sacred space. Doing this ritual by a body of water is also wonderful, though my personal preference is to do this ritual in a grounded sacred space and then immediately soak in a hot epsom salt bath, full of essential oils that support heart opening (such as rose, ylang-ylang, jasmine, and lavender).

Light your candle and focus on your intention to invoke sacred space. Say any prayers, or call in any spirit guides that feel supportive to your process.

Then, on a piece of paper draw out your heart compass. North, South, East and West. Place Love at the North with an infinity symbol underneath it. Write Love under the infinity symbol. South on the Compass is Courage. Draw an infinity symbol with the words Victory/Success below. West is the direction of Forgiveness. Draw an infinity symbol with the word Healing underneath. And lastly, the direction of the East is Gratitude. Draw an infinity symbol with the word Grace underneath it. You can get as simple or creative with this as you like.

Once you have your compass drawn out, place one hand on your heart and the other holding your compass. This ritual is a moving meditation. Ask your heart what direction she needs right now and see where on your paper compass you are guided. Physically stand in that direction, and see what intuitive messages or images come to you and then journal to integrate your experience.

Another way to work with this is to move through the whole compass, standing in each direction asking for wisdom and guidance in each quadrant. Be open to where your heart compass guides you.

Lastly, you can come to your compass as if she were an oracle. Ask her any question that is on your mind, or surrender a challenge or obstacle to her and see which direction she guides you in. You may be pleasantly surprised by the oracle of your heart!

Tapping into the energy of the heart can be quite emotional, so I encourage you to drink the water you've brought to the ritual. This will be cleansing and hydrating, but also help move an energy that came up during the ritual.

I love consecrating this heart compass exploration with a dip in the sea/pool/or a bathtub! Let your heart guide you and trust that there's nothing left for you to do after you've taken the heart guided action of your compass. You are loved, you are Love!

Sacrament 5:

Gather Your People

Re-membering

There was a time when we gathered around in the most ancient shape of all, the circle. Fire present, community as council, everyone with their rightful place in the order of things. We celebrated and supported. We touched and healed and midwifed each other without question.

There was a time when people weren't islands, but holy parts of a whole.

There was a time when asking for help wasn't seen as weak, and receiving it wasn't considered a luxury.

There was a time when the terms "friend" or "family" weren't ills to initiate psychotherapy, but the very antidotes to what plagued us in the first place.

There was a time when we held each other, deeply.

There was a time when we were loved for exactly who we were.

Remember this time.

Gather Your People

"It takes the time it takes...until you have the community."

— Sobonfu Somè

Send your flare out into the world

The first three Sacraments help us to make contact with the Truth of who we are. We slow down and honor our bodies so we can hear and feel for that Truth. We unapologetically rise into Sacrament 3 so that Truth can become strengthened and clarified without guilt or shame. We then move into the heart compass of Sacrament 4 so we can take aligned action based on that Truth in the world.

From this place of deep alignment, it is natural, then, to want to express our Truth. This expression can come from the things we literally say or write, but it's often in the way we choose to be; in other words, expressing ourselves through the choices we make, such as personal style, voting with our dollar, and how we educate our children.

Every time a woman expresses her Truth instead of following the status quo, it's like sending a solar flare out into the Universe attracting others who are doing the same. This expression of authenticity may call in others who are aligned with your specific Truth, and this bolsters your sense of belonging. It may also attract people who disagree with you but honor your capacity to embody your Truth anyway because it emboldens them to continue expressing theirs. In this way, gathering your people is ultimately about celebrating the underlying unity within diversity.

As such, I invite you to choose language for this Sacrament that feels most authentic to *you*. Depending upon the intersectionality of your unique race, ethnicity and upbringing, the sentiment of "your people" might feel more resonantly expressed as "tribe, clan, soul-family, circle, pack, flock, or simply community." As with all the Sacraments, there is no right or wrong way, there is simply your authentic way.

Whatever you choose to call "your people," be sure that the essence behind this Sacrament is this: : raise your freak flag, do you and be you, and the world will organize around that. From this place of radical authenticity we heal and evolve the wounds of patriarchy into Love.

This is NOT a Clique

Part of healing from the wound of patriarchy is releasing the paradigm of cliques and embracing the paradigm of your people. If you managed to survive middle school or high school without the pain of cliques, bless you. For most of us, however, there's been at least one painful instance in our lives, perhaps even in adulthood, where we felt outcast or alien because of clique dynamics.

Cliques appear to be your people, as they're groups of people who seemingly feel a sense of belonging together. The harmful current of cliques, however, is the current of cool. There's always something you need to have, or think, or do, or stop doing, in order to be cool and fit into the clique. In an instant, you can feel yourself outcasted if you didn't get the unspoken memo about what was defined as cool that day.

The current of cool is intimately woven with group-think. If you dare question that group-think, your sense of belonging is immediately threatened. Sometimes we're lucky enough to brush these moments off and move on, but the culture of cliques can often breed bullying and competition that leave indelible marks on our hearts for years to come.

Gathering your people, on the other hand, is the experience of having your sense of home reflected back to you in one or more people. When you are home inside yourself there's nowhere else you have to be or anything else to do, you're just you. In this way, you feel a homecoming with your people, because there's an energetic resonance with your innate being. The consciousness of your people doesn't ask you to prove anything or become something else in order to belong. Your people say, "We love you and want more of you; all the things that make you you, more of *that* please!"

Queens Don't compete, they celebrate

In the realm of Divine Feminine consciousness, we release the need to compete with other women and instead celebrate them. Gathering your people is about remembering that there's a seat at the table for everyone. When you find the ones that feel like home to you, then do everything in your power to elevate them. Celebrate the shit out of every woman you come into contact with. Even the bitchy ones, they clearly need it the most!

When a woman in your circle has a special talent or becomes successful she is not your competition, she is a model of what is also possible for you. Her love, her money, her good health are all yours too. The sign of a true Queen is a woman who helps another woman become successful. A true Queen understands that there's no one else on the planet just like her. Perhaps others wear the same professional titles, but no one can do what she does exactly like she does it. It is natural, then, for a successful woman to want other women to be successful, and to give them as many hot tips on how to get there along the way.

In fact, we are less likely to sabotage our success when we know we have a cheering squad of other women supporting us along the way. Plus, how good does it feel to lift up another woman? How good does it feel when others lift you up? True sisterhood is a feeling beyond any number that a dollar sign in your bank account could provide. Finding your people is the true currency of belonging because it doesn't cost you anything to access it.

You are not meant to do it alone. None of it. Reclaim your right to RECEIVE. Re-member, true receiving becomes possible when we're being true to ourselves, when we are BEING our Truest selves. Authenticity is the underpinning of Belonging. What was once impossible by yourself becomes possible through the power of togetherness.

Culture of I vs. We

At its core, Sacrament 5 is about un-doing the insidious patriarchal belief that we are weak if we ask for help, or desire support and connection with another. Although the first wave of Feminism was a necessary breakthrough for the collective, ironically it perpetuated a new psychological burden for women, "Because I can now do it all, I should do it all, by myself. This will make me a powerful, respectable, independent woman, worthy of the seat at the table I fought so hard to have."

However this limiting belief gets expressed in a woman, the end result is usually the same: exhaustion and burnout. Multiple generations now have martyred and exhausted themselves in the name of belonging. We think taking on more, overgiving and under-receiving will somehow garner us love and homecoming with others, but we betray our sense of self-belonging in the process. We try to find home outside of us in order to feel it inside, not knowing that the process actually works the other way around.

In this confusion, we forget how to ask for the very thing we need the most. Part of why we practice Sacrament 1 first is because in the slow, still place within, no matter how long it takes, a woman will eventually re-member how to howl for help.

It becomes imperative, then, to understand that most cultures around the world don't operate from this highly individualistic perspective, but instead, a collectivistic one. In other words, most other cultures value the "we," before the "I."

In fact, there is a symbiotic understanding that the "I" exists for the "we," and the "we" exists for the "I." There is no separation, there is no hierarchy, but instead a circular understanding of belonging. There are shadow sides to this cultural paradigm, as well, namely the experience of saving face or staying small in order to fit it, but trust that you can feel the difference in your own experience. You can feel it in your body when you are around your true people.

Imagine growing up in a culture where everyone inherently understood that giving and receiving support for all people in the community was actually what maintained the health of each individual therein. Imagine the impact on your mental and emotional health. Imagine the impact on your physical health, and how safe and secure you'd feel in the world. Imagine what it would feel like to receive this support without guilt. Imagine how respected you would feel by others for asking for help when you need it, and how good it would feel for others to provide it when you do.

You can choose this cultural shift within yourself right now. You can declare it as so. You can begin to evoke reciprocity as a tenet of all your relations, including the relationship you have with Self. You can do this without having to actually take on anyone else's culturally nuanced ways of expressing this reciprocity, either. But if you need some inspiration, call on the ones who came before you, your well and bright ancestors. They will whisper where to find your people and how to tend to that sacred connection.

Listen for the clues sprinkled throughout the songs, the seasonal rituals, the mythology, and oracular history of tending Mother Earth and Her bounty. Listen for the ancient medical practices and sexual rites. Listen for war time stories just as much as love time stories, for this will illuminate what your people valued and fought for, perhaps illuminating your very purpose here and now.

Dig Deeper

We are all indigenous to somewhere (and sometimes many somewheres). However, through waves of global colonialism, many of us have been divorced from our indigenous roots. "Our people" is a foreign concept.

My dear, I encourage you to dig deeper.

No matter the historical trauma or cycles of immigration your lineage survived, despite race, every woman can trace her way back to the roots of her people of origin. Perhaps your DNA has multiple points of origin, but to be sure, you come from somewhere. Researching the bloodlines you come from and the ancient ways of relating and belonging these peoples practiced will fortify your capacity for relating to yourself with greater clarity, authenticity, integrity and pride. This then fortifies your capacity to do the same with others.

If possible, I encourage you to take pilgrimages to the physical lands your people come from. When you reconnect the spiritual umbilical cord between you and Motherland in this way, you will re-member a deeper understanding of belonging in your body. This, too, is homecoming.

Maybe you don't uproot your current life to move back to your Motherland, but you no longer feel so lost because you've touched down with the original home. You're no longer running away from it. In doing so you close an energetic loop that got opened when your ancestors left. In doing so, you give yourself the gift of understanding your place in the greater order of things. You can then call on the frequency of that place and those people whenever you need, and their wisdom will guide and inspire you.

Gathering your people feels less daunting because you've remembered the original blueprint of how to do it.

The flock you came from may not be the flock you fly with... and that is OK

Finding your people can feel like a tricky thing if you grew up feeling like the black sheep of your family. No matter how hard you try you may never think, act, or see the world the way they do and vice versa.

This can feel deeply confusing when we're programmed to believe that our biological family of origin is the place where we should feel most at home in the world. But if you've always felt like a humming-bird amongst geese, then it's probably because you're meant to learn something from the geese that fortifies your ability to fly with the other hummingbirds.

In other words, as painful as it might be at times, the challenging dynamics we experience with our family of origin can be exactly the things we need to illuminate where we want to make a change in the world. As human beings, we tend to learn through contrast, and I know no more intimate and immediate contrast than that of family dynamics to accelerate our learning.

The flock you come from illuminates your purpose, and the flock you fly with is the circle of other change-makers here to help you fulfill that purpose. It could be easy to cast our family of origin as assholes, but even if extreme boundaries need to be put in place, see if on some level you can tap back into Sacrament 4, cultivate gratitude where possible, and then welcome in the grace. The grace may be that you can finally hold the paradox that although you love your family, you don't actually like them, and acknowledging this brings you peace. Or the grace may be that life blesses you with an abundance of Soul family this lifetime, connecting you with your people all over the world.

To be sure, though, the pain from where we don't feel connected to others will always point us in the direction of the places where we do. Don't fall into the trap of blaming others or wishing they were different, this will waste your precious energy. Just be the hummingbird and keep flying until you find your flock.

Hyper self-reliance is a trauma response

Your healing lies in your capacity to learn how to receive. If you grew up in a system (familial, political, religious, or otherwise,) in which asking for what you needed was routinely denied, dismissed or mocked, you may have learned to stop asking for what you needed.

In fact, you may have learned to stop having needs at all. You may have learned that if one should arise, you were the only person who could or should tend to it.

On the outside looking in, women who employ hyper self-reliance often appear to be the strong women who have their shit together, the women others praise or aspire to be; the CEO's, the teachers, the leaders of the community who seemingly have it all. To be clear, it's a beautiful thing to be resourceful and create life for yourself. Much of our personal confidence and self-esteem come from achieving our goals. But if we swing the pendulum too far in either direction we run the risk of indebting ourselves from overgiving and depriving ourselves from under-receiving.

To have needs doesn't make you defective, it makes you human. When we acknowledge our humanity, we begin to heal the wounds rooted in our trauma. When we begin to practice healthy ways of giving and receiving, we move out of programmed models of co-dependency and into interdependence. Not only does this feel better, we can actually achieve more, ironically enough.

What felt impossible on our own, becomes possible through the help of others.

Keep in mind that your people can truly be just one other person. Think of how many lives would be saved if they knew they had one person they could call in a time of need. Gathering your people isn't defined by quantity, it's defined by quality of resonance. Let go of trying to do it all on your own and let in the LOVE that's here to help you.

Wild Woman

Because gathering your people upholds the tenet of authenticity, it inherently connects us to our wild self.

Wild, in this sense, is not crazy or out of control, but wild as in the most natural, primal, organic expression of self. Our wildness is like a river, around the right people it just flows. Life is challenging enough, be willing to let go of those who would try to dam your river. Seek those, instead, who make you pee your pants with laughter, encourage your loudness, and expand your audacity, joy, and plea-sure. You know, the ones who want to know how good your orgasm felt, or the rush from speaking your truth to your boss. The ones who rally for your fullest aliveness. Being around them is straight up healing technology, a sacred rebellion in a world that profits from your pain.

You are worthy of your wild.

Uncomfortable but honest

Your people won't be concerned with being nice, but with being real. They will call you out on your shit, shine a light on your shadow, and invite you to take responsibility for your life. Know that this is coming from a place of Love, because our people want the most for us. All humans have blindspots. This is natural. A truly good friend will help us lift the veil so we can see what's been blocking our breakthrough.

This may look like reflecting back to you that they see you repeating a familiar romantic pattern with your new partner, or sabotaging yourself from making progress on a goal. They may challenge a limiting belief you have, or set a boundary around a damaging behavior they want no part in. Although these moments may feel confrontational, thank them. These are acts of love.

Ultimately, you're a sovereign adult and can do whatever you want with their reflections. However, try taking some time to sit with the reflection from your friend and feel for where there is some truth or merit to what they're saying. It may just be the thing that unlocks the key to your liberation, catapulting you into the more of you!

Mirror Neurons: the power of "me, too."

Part of gathering your people may happen beneath your level of awareness. You simply being you may change the course of someone's life who rode the subway or ran through the park with you that day. Maybe you're a public figure, and speaking your truth on television or a local speech you made saved a life. We positively impact a sense of belonging for people all the time without ever knowing it.

Think then how even more powerful it is to create this change when we *are* aware of it. One way we do this is by telling our stories.

Many of us have been socialized that telling our personal stories is dramatic, self-indulgent, or inappropriate. Nine times out of ten, however, when we tell our stories, it gives other women permission to tell theirs. When we see ourselves reflected in the story of another woman who also went through a deep challenge, it gives us hope for our own resiliency. When we hear the story of a woman who achieved the thing we're actively working on, it provides momentum to cross the finish line.

When we see ourselves reflected in another woman's story, we remember we are not alone. And this is everything. It is more powerful than any pill or well-researched therapy could provide. The power of "me, too," provides an immediate balm to the psyche of a woman, which in turn provides endurance for the process of her homecoming.

Include the unseen realm

When you gather your people, you're not just calling on the friends, family and mentors of blood and flesh, you're also inviting all the unseen support of other realms: your ancestors, guardian angels, spirit guides, the fae, gnomes, earth elementals, and other benevolent energies here to support your highest and best. This also includes songs, poems, and other works of art that help you remember who the fuck who you are.

Remember, gathering your people is the experience of feeling home with another, so feel free to be creative about your interpretation of who that other is!

The Circle

The most ancient shape and symbol in our universe is the circle. Since the beginning of time, people have gathered in circles to embody both the sacred and the mundane aspects of life; everything from eating around the fire, to calling in deep healing around the fire. Throughout the course of history women have gathered in circles to connect, create, heal, and transform.

The circle is the place of alchemy and magic. It is the place of witnessing and being witnessed without judgment. It is the sacred place of sanctuary from the world. It is the "red tent," that marks a woman's rite of passage through all her life stages, especially her menstrual cycle.

In modern day, women's circles of all kinds, physical and virtual, exist around the world, but no matter the format, the energy and intention is the same. By its very nature, the circle is non-hierarchical. As such, every woman in a circle has a place and a voice.

If finding your people feels challenging, call out to the circles of women who've come before you and watch for their guidance on how to find your circle now. With an open Heart Compass leading the way, oftentimes the circle will find you first.

When leaves fall

You may notice that, as you come more into alignment with the truth of who you are, people who no longer match that frequency may fall away from your life.

You may even internalize this as you having done something wrong. No, my love, that's the old you, the good-girl-people-pleaser rearing her self-protective head again. Take a deep breath and breathe into the discomfort of letting go.

Queens understand that the process of homecoming requires letting go of everything that isn't home, in order to come into alignment with what is. It's just the nature of things, like leaves falling in Autumn to prepare for new growth in Spring.

By definition, our growth and expansion expands us. Those who feel threatened by our expansion or afraid of their own won't be able to tolerate being in our presence. This isn't good or bad, it's just energy. Maybe your interests and hobbies have changed and theirs stayed the same. Or a belief structure of yours shifted, and theirs didn't. Try holding the awareness that none of this is right or wrong, everyone is on their own journey.

It can be painful to lose people we love, but it's often more painful to try and be old versions of ourselves around them. Staying in relationships that no longer feel generative isn't loving, it's often rooted in a sense of obligation or scarcity. We might fear what will happen if we let the relationship go, we might worry there won't be a more aligned relationship to fill that place. When we come home to ourselves, we inherently know that we are enough, and that there is enough in the world.

A former client once said to me, "A smart woman knows when to leave something that no longer serves her, or others." Remember Sacrament 4, Love lets go. Even if it feels like the rug is being ripped out from under you and you have no choice in the matter, you can often look back to see the Loving hand guiding your path away from what was ultimately harmful or unhealthy.

Allow for the full spectrum of emotions to arise as you experience this. Losing some people may bring up a lot of grief, while others bring a sense of peace or relief. Trust what comes up, give it space to move through you, and then set the table for the new, higher aligned Love to come in.

A heretic for Love

Many people genuinely find a sense of belonging in religious communities. Let's celebrate and elevate this where it is actually true. However, the experience of church can also be fraught with deep pain. Everything from clique-like middle school manipulation to fit in or else, to outright abuse can take place under the guise of "God." To question the church, to think critically for oneself, or to want a spiritual connection filled with more sensuality or authenticity can quickly exile a member out of "belonging."

In case you need to hear this: You are allowed to have any relationship with the Divine you want to. It's *your* relationship, and no one else's. It may trigger others' belief structures or internalized oppression, but don't you dare dampen your authentic connection to the Divine because it makes others feel uncomfortable. If you're coming from a place of genuine Love and desire to connect with whatever you call God, that's all that matters.

For every man-made church you may be kicked out of, there will be ten times more moments of Love, Joy, and Healing you'll receive in your direct gnosis with God Herself; your body and the Earth are the conduits, no preachers or priests required. Be the witch they tried to burn 300 hundred years ago and then watch them burn with envy for a freedom they don't yet dare claim for themselves. Your coven of sister-witches will find you.

Personal Story:

When we gather our people, we invoke our return to the most ancient symbol of all, the circle. There is nothing a woman cannot accomplish with a circle of seen and unseen support by her side.

My journey with disordered eating began at age 10. I experienced bulimia throughout college and my early 20's, mostly addicted to laxatives and other purgatives. I couldn't reconcile my deep knowing of food as sacred and my body as holy, with the societal and familial pressures to look a certain way. Like most high-achieving, type-A "good girls," I was excellent at hiding this part of my life and pretending that I was happy. Whenever I was asked about my weight loss or complimented on it, I pretended like I hadn't noticed, or that I wasn't doing anything other than "just being healthy."

This level of dishonesty was so painful, let alone the physical pain I was in for a really long time. Hello gut-healing journey!

I'd been at war with my body longer than I hadn't, and even though I was exhausted, I literally didn't know any other way. Then, the choice of no-choice arrived on my doorstep. Like it always did before I knew about the Sacraments.

It was the summer before moving to San Francisco for grad school and I was on family vacation at the beach. At the end of the trip, my uncle let slip that my grandmother had made some snide remark about my step-mother's body, and that I wasn't excluded from those body-shaming comments either. Angered at my uncle's chronic lack of tact, and totally grief-stricken that my own grandmother would be so cruel and judgemental, I hit an emotional point of no return.

Just a few months prior, I had found myself dehydrated and hanging over a toilet, not feeling I had enough energy to even crawl my way back to bed. Did anyone know how much I was wrecking myself every day to fit some impossible standard? I was either going to die trying, or I was finally going to get help. And try to get some fucking help for the insidious ways Patriarchy incites women judging and shaming other women!

The next day, I confronted my father and asked if I could speak to him in private. It took everything in me to utter the words, "I need help." I divulged to him that I had been addicted to laxatives, and had been struggling with some form of disordered eating for years. There weren't many words exchanged, but many, many tears. My dad, having always been a proponent of my brother and I seeking mental health support since my parents' divorce, immediately offered to pay for therapy or any other kind of support I needed once I got to San Francisco. I was grateful. I was relieved. I had no idea what that support looked like, but now I was accountable for receiving it, and accountable for finally laying this cycle to rest.

Most of my family never knew I had an eating disorder. So when my step-father challenged me to run a half-marathon in my first semester of grad school, I was presented with a really interesting choice. Was I going to run to lose weight or was I going to run for something else this time?

I remember consciously making the decision to sign up for this half marathon so that I might know in this lifetime what it feels like to be in my body simply for the joy of it. To run for my strength. To run for my health. To run for my freedom from everything that had ever weighed me down.

As fate would have it, my first apartment in San Francisco was just a few blocks from Golden Gate Park. If I ran to and through the park and back it was nearly a 7 mile loop, Ocean Beach being the halfway point. I'd never been able to run to the ocean before, so on a whim I decided this would be my training loop.

I'll never forget the first time I did this run. I got to Golden Gate Park and, within minutes, began to notice something different. This was not what running in Los Angeles looked like. This was not being surrounded by skinny actors and actresses at Emerson College. These were not pubescent cheerleaders in high school. This was WOMAN. For what felt like literally the first time in my life, I saw other women who looked like me. I saw women who were tall, thick, strong, curvy, brave and bold. I saw muscles, I saw cellulite, I saw stretch marks, I saw juicy fucking booties that were rockin' it! I saw women much larger than me letting it all hang out. I saw pride. I saw joy. I saw acceptance. I saw the possibility of living in a world where all was welcome. Including me.

I also saw fucking Bison! For real, in case y'all didn't know, there's a whole herd of Bison just hanging out in Golden Gate Park. These motherfuckers don't mess around. And if I ever forgot who I was, I'd get to the Bison park and remember. Period. Solid, unapologetic, bodies and forces of nature they were.

Imagine, I was 26 years old and I'd never seen a body like mine. Or, I was never allowed to see a body like mine in the same space as that body being celebrated. I had only ever experienced a body like mine being judged, made fun of, or questioned-surely your dad can't be your dad with an ass like that, Sarah, are you sure you're really White? Oh yeah, my body and racial identity were often a topic of conversation in school. Don't even get me started.

The point is, mirror neurons. The simple act of seeing my own reflection is what kickstarted my recovery from an eating disorder. Week in and week out I ran with random strangers for miles in San Francisco. But something in me knew that we all knew we were running for, and with, each other. My shift in body image was not only bolstered by an increase in strength and endurance from all the running, I was also finally living in a city that valued eating the way I'd always intuitively been called to eat. This was reflected in every grocery store or neighborhood corner store, but it was also reflected in the choices my friends and colleagues were making. Eating health-fully wasn't some weird trend or a cover for a disorder, it was a genuine act of reverence for the body and the Earth. It was common for my friends and I to have gorgeous potlucks full of healthy food that we prayed over. This prayer shifted the molecules of the food, how my body digested it, and most importantly my relationship to it.

Grad school was also the first time I felt like I was surrounded by my people in the sense of consciousness; finally people who thought, felt, and perceived the world the way I did. I was not some freak, I was me, in a sea of other brilliant human beings who dared to be them-selves as well. We were not here to participate in the status quo matrix, we were here to disrupt it, heal the remnants of it, and build a new one from the ground up.

In those days, the gathering of my people was less of a conscious calling-in and more of a daily fortification from my environment. I never went to a therapist or an eating disorder clinic to seek treatment. I went to the woods, the ocean, and to the sacred circles of my community. I went deep into my heart and the soles of my feet. I went deep into the root of the root of how this all started in the first place, which had nothing to do with food, and everything to do with core childhood wounds.

As I noticed just how supported I was by my people unconsciously, I began practicing the calling in of my people consciously, calling on friends, family or spirit guides when I needed. The healing of my body was also the beginning of my spiritual awakening, and I found that the deepest connection to spirit, for me, always, and I mean always, brought me back to my body.

I started dancing at age 3, and I think somehow I always knew that's where I'd return to. This is why I dance and teach Qoya. This is why I run. This is why I incorporate yoga and breathwork into everything I do. I've come to understand and embody that core Magdalene tenant, which is that ascension isn't about transcending anything, it's about going deeper inside. And for me, it's not just deeper into the heart, it's deeper into every cell of my body.

I can honestly say that when I stand in front of a mirror now, I genuinely love every inch of me. This did not happen overnight, and there were many moments of two steps forward one step back, disordered eating masquerading as other "symptoms." But at age 35 I truly get it now. I am a miracle, all ten fingers, all ten toes. Motherfucking MIRACLE.

I could not know this so deep in my bones if I had not had my people (seen and unseen) relentlessly reflecting this back to me again, and again, and again.

Representation matters. Body image and eating disorders affect every gender, race, sexual orientation, ethnicity, socio-economic status, and religion. Find your people, and don't let go. Even if right now that's just Lizzo's instagram account. Queen, that too, is gathering your people. That too, is sacred support. Receive it. You are not alone. You are worthy of support forever and always, and in all ways. Use your throat chakra to send a flare into the universe and DECLARE IT SO. HERE AND NOW.

I'll meet you in the park, next to the Bison. Together we will cast a circle that shall never be broken.

Practicing Sacrament 5
Overview

Shadow: Sisterhood wound, the Mean Girl archetype, cliques, etc. There can also be a tendency towards inflexibility or lack of adaptability with the Other, those who are NOT your people. Just remember, you don't have to like everyone, and everyone doesn't have to like you; gathering your people enables you to be fortified when life requires you to be around Others. This is balance, and this provides great learning along the path. How boring would it be if everyone were the same?!

Chakra: This Sacrament is connected to the 5th Chakra which is located at the throat. As such, anytime you touch, activate or make sounds from this part of your body you're practicing this Sacrament. This chakra radiates the color frequency of blue. It's important to note that the concept of "our people" is typically attributed to the 1st chakra in many traditions, the chakra connected to the ground, our roots, our family and ancestors. However, in the Sacraments of the Goddess, gathering our people is connected to our throat chakra because belonging to others can only happen when we truly belong to ourselves first (this is the work of the first four sacraments.)

199

Only from this place of true self-belonging can we literally use our throat to call-in others who vibrate at the same frequency we do. This is crucial to our healing, emotionally and neurobiologically (remember my personal story in Sacrament 5 related to mirror neurons). This chakra is deeply connected to the release of self-censorship and concealing of Truth in exchange for the development of healthy self-expression.

Earth Cycles

Moon phases: During the New Moon, use your throat chakra to voice or write down your intentions related to relationships in your life. In the corresponding Full Moon (usually 6 months later), revisit these intentions and take stock of your relationships.

The New Moon phase can also be a powerful time to use your voice for declaring what relationships you're willing to release so that more aligned ones can come in. This includes the realm of love and romance. As such, I love doing good old-fashioned "love spells" on the New Moon to call-in Love in all the ways! I often like to do this by a fire or a body of water so the elements can witness and alchemize my prayer! Our lovers and beloveds are our people too, no? Have fun! And likewise, if you're mending a broken heart, this Sacrament can be a powerful practice for declaring love for Self. The more we engage in positive self-love and self-expression, the more Love, in all its forms, can find us, without an ounce of striving or desperation on our part!

Seasons: There is never not a season to gather your people!

Although we typically think of this Sacrament during the Fall and Winter seasons where we're celebrating the harvest or gathering for the holy holidays, Spring and Summer are equally times of community celebration. Whatever your personal cultural, religious or spiritual traditions are, the key to embracing this Sacrament with each seasonal turn of the wheel comes down to one word: *intentionality*.

If we approach communing with others as a sacred act, then we intentionally prepare for it. This brings a level of care and tending to the space created that enables everyone present to feel safe, welcomed, and included. It also creates an experience that reflects back to you your values, even if the "gathering" is a voice memo exchange or a Zoom chat.

In other words, when we gather with our people, we're not going through the motions or doing what we've always done for tradition's sake; we gather with intentionality and this creates a truly sacred, sensual, sovereign experience that honors the Truth of who we are, in ways subtle or grand.

Supports

Mantras:

- I am not meant to do this alone.
- I am worthy of receiving support.
- I gather my people and the impossible becomes possible.
- All dreams are made manifest with support.
- Speaking my Truth is alchemy.
- My voice matters; my sounds are sacred.
- My truest self-expression draws the right people into my life.
- I am abundantly supported by the Universe when I speak my Truth.
- My clear communication creates ripples of healing.
- I express myself with ease.
- Calling in my community is a sign of strength, not weakness.
- I am wild.
- I am a feral woman who runs with a pack of sacred, sensual, sovereign sisters, so don't fuck with me!
- My voice is a sacred declaration.

Divine Feminine allies:

- Spider Woman
- Gaia, Pachamama, Mama Pacha, Terra

Herbal ally: Lavender

- Lavender soothes the pain and depression that comes from

hiding who we are. She gently calms the insecurities we feel when we risk speaking out loud our true thoughts, beliefs, feelings, and dreams. Be seen and heard with lavender and send your frequency out into the world!

- This herb can be ingested through teas, tinctures, flower essences, infused honey and elixirs. It can also be topically applied in hydrosol mists, lotions or body sprays. It's also a beautiful herbal ally to burn in oil diffusers or in incense form. However, simply meditating on this herb can bring powerful insight and awareness.

Songs:

- "O,Sister" by Woven Kin
- "Bone by Bone" by Marya Stark
- "Howl" by Florence + The Machine
- "I Wanna Be Like You" (feat. Sea-Ren) by KR3TURE
- "We Are Family" by Sister Sledge

Integration tools:

WORDS ARE SPELLS. Cast them consciously, clearly, and LOVINGLY. You will then receive people and experiences in your life that reflect back this clear, conscious LOVE. Be patient. This takes time. We're programmed by society for scarcity/negativity/lack. Casting spells of Love & Abundance might feel more challenging than you thought. This is ok. This is normal. Practice. Keep going. You're not alone. We're literally creating a new Earth *together*!

Sing. It does NOT matter what you sound like. Singing in the car or shower is just as healing and valuable as singing on stage. You're singing for YOU and no one else. You are singing for your liberation. You are singing your people home to you!

Chant / Mantra. If you have specific chants or mantras connected to your spiritual practice, by all means continue with those practices. If chanting or mantra is new to you, I suggest a simple "I AM LOVED" (or any of the mantras listed above) 10 times in a row, then see how you feel.

Affirmations. Spoken or written. If written, post them throughout your home or car!

Ask for help. Practice calling your friends and *asking for help* with something even if, and particularly when, it's uncomfortable or vulnerable.

Give compliments. Compliment someone or speak a gratitude for them for no particular reason, and then watch this generous energy boomerang back to you tenfold in unexpected ways!

Gather. Create a women's circle or sacred gathering, outdoors or any place your heart guides you. (Please honor your own comfort levels with this during Covid.)

Release. Do a burn ritual or grief ceremony to support the continued release of sister-wounds from childhood or adulthood. Doing this WITH another friend amplifies the healing through the act of being witnessed. My favorite is the *"Sacred Rage Ceremony"* where my best friend and I put on super primal music, light candles, burn essential oils, dim the lights, open the windows, and then beat the shit out of a couch with some pillows! We cry, we scream, we growl and howl, and usually we end up in a fit of laughter together. It's pure medicine, and a powerful portal for LETTING THAT SHIT GO!

Call your people in. Write out or speak out the kind of people you would like to call into your life. Get nitty gritty with the details. The Universe loves clarity!

Visualize. Envision yourself in a sacred site or place in nature. Meditate on how you feel in that place, the sense of home, safety, belonging, communion and community with the land/water/etc. Then, visualize your people (even if it's just one other person) joining you in that space. In your journal, write down what you say to each other in this place. How does this place feel? What do you and your people do together here? Then ask your Soul how you can bring this experience into your day to day life with people you love, or people that you are calling in to your reality.

Let people go. Sounds simple, but this is actually the most important part of this Sacrament. We cannot welcome our true people if old relationships that no longer serve us are blocking the way. Make peace with lovers, exes, friends that no longer resonate, family members who have passed or who don't honor who you are/respect your boundaries, etc. Make this letting go a ritual. Write a letting go letter and place it in a body of water or bury it in the ground. Let Mama Earth transmute it for you.

BELIEVE. Knowing that you're worthy of populating your life with healthy, kind, loving, generous, resonant relationships is honestly 50% of the equation. From this belief, all becomes possible. It's just a matter of Divine Timing before these new, nourishing relationships reveal themselves to you. Allow yourself to be surprised by the forms your people come in!

Invocations

Prayer:

Divine Mother, I call on You to witness the Wild Woman in me rise! Through your Love and protection, I am guided to speak my Truth clearly and boldly in the world. My healthy self-expression sends a rally call out into the Universe for my people to find me.

Through Your Grace, those who need to fall away, fall away, and those who are ready to come, may come.

I am surrounded by like-hearted people who mirror back to me my values, self-worth, sacred boundaries, and aspirations. My people support the fullest expression of me, and I support the fullest expression of them.

Through the divine reciprocity of true family, I heal all wounds related to giving and receiving, and come into right relation with the frequency of support. I am worthy of support. I am worthy of community. I belong, I have always belonged, I will always belong. There is never not belonging, just my choice to choose it.

Thank you, Divine Mother, for this remembering.

Journal prompts:

Self, Relationships, Earth

Homecoming

Sarah Grady, MA

Maiden, Mother, Crone

Homecoming

Free write

Elemental release and reclaim ceremony

This Sacrament is connected to the element of AIR. As such, I recommend doing the burn ceremony from Sacrament 1, but replacing the language of "Slowing Down" with any words related to gathering your people, community, soul family, etc. Using your voice aloud and in written form to burn away any beliefs you have around belonging or past wounds around not belonging in any way is such a powerful activation and healing for your throat chakra and 5th Sacrament.

Feel free to revisit that ritual any time you're struggling in your relationships. It will recharge your self-belonging and invoke forgiveness so the path be made clear for the highest aligned people to find you in every facet of life.

In addition to the burn ceremony, I highly suggest a ritual, inspired by my dear sister-friend Aylah, entitled "Wolf in Sheep's Clothing."

You'll want to gather the following items: a candle, a black cloth/scarf/old shirt that you don't mind never seeing again, stones, shells or other earth items you can write on, a black sharpie, red yarn to tie up your bundle with and your favorite outfit, preferably something with Red in it to symbolize your connection to the red thread of the Divine Feminine. This thread weaves all women together through the red of our monthly blood cycle.

Set aside dedicated time and space to go into ritual. Light your candle, call in any spirit guides or allies, and invoke the frequency of the wolf—both the distorted predatory wolf, and the healthy wolf that fiercely loves and protects her pack.

Homecoming

For the first part of the ritual, write down any relationship in your life that was an experience of a wolf in sheep's clothing (i.e. someone who presented to be one way and then turned out to be completely different). Then write out any time you were the wolf in sheep's clothing. This can be hard and humbling, but so healing to do. Perhaps you pretended to be something you weren't to fit in in high school or with your family, or maybe you put on a facade in exchange for the illusion of love with a lover. The externalization of this is helpful for releasing any shame attached to it. We've all done it, and now it's time to let it go.

Once you've written an exhaustive list, find a way to distill this into one or two words (or even just a name) that you can write in sharpie on your rocks, shells, etc. Once complete, gather all your rocks into the black piece of fabric and tie it up with the yarn.

Take this bundle to a body of water or to a plot of earth where you can bury it. As you submerge this bundle in the water or soil simply chant, sing, whisper or pray the words "Rest In Peace."

Do this as many times as you need until you feel an energetic shift internally. Your body will tell you when this is complete. Return to your ritual space and put on your favorite outfit that makes you feel like a million bucks! Then turn on your favorite playlist or song on repeat and SING, dance, cry, and whatever else you need to do. Just be sure to breathe so the air element can continue to cleanse and clear this pattern of wolf in sheep's clothing.

Then, when you're ready, you can speak or sing your intention to call your people home to you. Whether that's a prayer for new, higher-aligned friendships, co-workers, collaborators, or healed relationships with family members or neighbors, sound your vocal flare up into the sky and call in the pack of healthy wolves you're meant to run with.

In working with the wolf energy of belonging to a pack, I'm often reminded that the people who most see us and love us in life are also connected to our wild, primal nature. We don't have to be anything but our organic selves with them. As such, any ritual that invokes your wild woman nature will be an act of Gathering Your People. Howl at the moon, put your bare feet on the earth, swim naked in the ocean, rub soil on your face, get your hands dirty or pour your menstrual blood into the earth. All of this invokes your connection to your primal, authentic self, and directly or indirectly calls your primal pack to you. Have fun, my feral sister!

Sacrament 6:

Above All Else, Trust Yourself

Re-membering

There was a time when we didn't question what we were guided to do because we understood that we were being guided by something larger and much wiser than us. We understood how to decipher the codes of that source through our bodies, and we trusted those messages without question.

This is how we planted and harvested our food "on time."

This is how women made, gestated and birthed babies.

This is how we survived trauma and crisis.

There were less distractions and more time for awareness. Women's intuitive ways of knowing were revered as gifts, not threats.

This knowing is how we survived, and it is also how we thrived.

Remember this time.

Above All Else, Trust Yourself

"You know, like you know a good watermelon."

— Mary Justus

Permission slips

You know. In your bones, you *know*. Stop backpedaling or pretending like you don't. You do.

Remember sacrament 3 and let go of how you think others will respond to your knowing. Their reaction is not your responsibility. Listening to your soul and living in integrity *is* your responsibility. Every time you trust yourself and move in that direction, you give another woman a permission slip to do the same. Go on now, start your revolution.

Just do it

We practice the first three sacraments so we can feel for our truth and align with it unapologetically. We then move up into the 4th Sacrament so our truth can be guided by the Loving wisdom of the heart. We call on Sacrament 5 to support this alignment process when needed, but ultimately we must move in the direction of our own, sovereign knowing. Once you've aligned with your truth and garnered support where necessary, there really is nothing to it but to do it, and to *trust*. Trust that you have all the skills, information, or resources to do what you need to do. No more planning or thinking, just trust yourself and go.

Trust yourself, because we live in a world that doesn't want you to

Ultimately, the current order of things profits off of women staying small, outsourcing their knowledge and power onto people, namely men. Sure, there will always be people who know more about a subject than you do, but this doesn't mean you have no knowing. Don't allow anyone else's perceived qualifications to overshadow that which already lives inside you. Every time you rise above those critical voices of not good enough and choose to trust yourself, you ultimately send a signal to the world that *you are home*. You are a woman who is turned on, and fully occupies her being.

The irony, of course, is that even though the system of patriarchy doesn't want you to trust yourself, it ultimately respects and rewards you way more if you do. The signal is clear: you are not a doormat, you are Joan of Arc of your own storyline, and you've got mountains to move.

What does trust feel like in your body?

When we trust someone or something, we often say it "just feels right." Start to get curious about what this feeling actually feels like. Is it solid, light, warm, expansive, rooted, freeing, tingly, etc.? Trust feels slightly different to everyone. Start to cultivate your personal definition and be willing to allow it to evolve over time as you grow your relationship to it.

Trust is a feeling called follow-through

Self-trust is ultimately about tracking the reoccurring thoughts, feelings, and intuitive messages you receive about something, and then taking action based on that inner information. If you keep getting the same vision, message, or download again and again, it's usually for a reason, so trust it!

You are not crazy; life is trying to get your attention. As we know from the guidance of our heart compass, the messages we get may not always make "sense," in the moment, but we can often understand the wisdom in them hindsight.

Taking action based on our inner knowing is ultimately like flexing a muscle. The more you do it, the easier it becomes to do. A woman new to self-trust may need to start small and routinely give herself permission. This is OK. Be where you are.

Over time, however, the process of self-trust becomes like jumping off a diving board; exhilarating second nature to a swimmer. And my dear, if you've read this far, you ain't no wallflower. You are a sacred swimmer of life, intent on her homecoming.

So *trust*.

You do not need another degree, your certificates won't save you

My love, you are more brilliant than all the stars in the galaxy. You have profound intelligence and wisdom living inside your bones. This brilliance came into existence the day you were born.

To be sure, your systemic educational experiences have shaped you. You've acquired new knowledge and skill sets, that married with your innate intelligence, propelled you into greater knowing. This is beautiful, but none of the degrees or certificates you've accumulated are genuine reflections of your worth or your authority on knowing what's best for yourself.

In this data driven, achievement-oriented culture of patriarchy, it is a sacred rebellion to remember that you are credible, *because you exist.* The rat race of higher education and never-ending acquisition of pieces of paper to prove yourself have got to stop. Please trust that you have all the information inside you to make decisions for yourself. When you feel like you don't, gather your people and ask for sound counsel. Then sit with what you receive and filter it through your own channel.

Practice Sacraments 1 and 2 to really hear the whispers. No matter how long it takes, you will come to a knowing, and you will know it as knowing by the way it *feels.* To trust yourself is to follow the feeling from within. This is where your inner masculine and feminine energies truly synergize to make shit happen in life, and I know you know how damn good *that* feels.

When you feel wobbly, remind yourself of all the times you trusted yourself and it worked out. Invoke the memory of those miracles, milestones and blessings; they will bolster you with boldness and courage when you need it most. Then make your own damn degree and hang it on the wall. In bold red letters may it read, "I'm a badass woman who trusts herself, Ph.D."

Ways of Knowing

Before modern technology, more intuitive ways of perceiving the world were employed to advance life; our instinct and intuition were the primary barometers for how we sourced food, birthed babies, built homes, and created safety. Some call these intuitive skill sets the *wise woman way*, being psychic, or the woman's 6th sense. There are commonly 4 ways of tapping into this wisdom. Some women have access to all four, or are more strongly gifted in one or two. Some gifts come in seasons and cycles. Regardless of how they come to you, don't dismiss them. Create loving, nonjudgmental space for these experiences to flow, inviting them to serve the highest alignment of yourself, or those seeking your guidance.

Clairaudience: the ability to *hear* psychic intuitive messages.

Claircognizance: the ability to receive intuitive *thoughts*; knowing information without knowing how or why you know it.

Clairvoyance: the ability to *see* psychic intuitive visions.

Clairsentience: the ability to *feel* psychic information.

Innervision/Innerstanding: To be clear, all four ways of psychically perceiving reality will be *inner* experiences you have, often with particular sensations attached to them, such as chills, goosebumps, temperature changes, or a pit in the stomach, etc. Your body is usually the first place to experience and express these ways of knowing before your conscious mind comes online to decipher and decode the messages received from the experience. Being psychic is not something relegated to a tarot reader at a carnival, it's a universal skill that we all have access to if we choose it.

No matter how soulful or spiritual (or NOT) a woman considers herself to be, every woman has had an experience when an inner knowing saved her life. Perhaps her gut told her to take a different route home from work than she usually does, only to discover later on the news that a deadly accident occurred on her usual route. Or for seemingly no good reason, she decides to back out of the contract for her dream home, only to later discover a toxic mold issue that went undetected by the inspector.

Healing the Witch Wound

Throughout the course of history, women who have accessed these ways of knowing and used them for healing have traditionally been outcasted from society. At best, these women were exiled from the community, at worst they were tortured and killed, often under the label of witch. The memory of the witch hunts live on in many of us today who dare to speak up and out about our Truth, or dare to live a life beyond the status quo.

The result of this is often much self-censoring or even paranoia, in the name of self-protection. This can also be the experience of taking two steps forward and one step back, not fully allowing yourself to succeed or shine. This trauma response is understandable, and yet, you also know you desire something beyond it. When you feel yourself stuck in a cycle, afraid to trust your knowing, the prescription is this: gather your people, get in your body, grieve, move the energy any way you feel called to, and then ask your Soul to remember the *herstory* that preceded *history*. Ask to remember the time on the planet when the priestesses and temple keepers trained at a high level to consciously and responsibly access and employ the gifts of knowing that women later got burned for. Resurrect the ancient one in you who walked those temple grounds and was abundantly supported by her community for doing so. Resurrect the herbalist, the sacred prostitute, the bodyworker, the artist, the healer and the midwife. Resurrect all the ones inside you and all the ones who came before you. Call all of the empowered feminine back into your bones and re-member who the fuck you are. When you do, they will not be able to touch or tame you. They will be begging you for more.

The world needs you. She needs all of you. Rise up.

Personal Stories

Trust yourself, because the whole world is rooting for you to know the miracle that exists on the other side of that trust.

Before I consciously knew about the Sacraments, I used this particular Sacrament as my go-to for making big life decisions, particularly moving all over the country, and the world.

One such moment was right after college graduation. I graduated a semester early, healthy overachiever, and suddenly found myself unemployed and in the unknown in what would've typically been my "Christmas Break." It was December of 2007 and I'd just completed a "semester abroad" in Los Angeles. Which frankly felt fucking foreign as hell to me, since I'd never been farther west than Chicago at that point. In this wild west semester, I studied film and television, and met one of my first Earth Angels of Los Angeles, my production professor, Marie Colabelli. A woman sent from the stars. She's from Philly and is also a dancer, so we were pretty kindred from the start. There was a sense that no matter what twists and turns life took me on from her class, we'd always be weaving a larger web together.

Fielding everyone's future-based questions during the holidays propelled me deep into contemplation and manifestation mode: what the actual fuck was I doing with my life?

Being a Yankee transplant raised in the South, I knew I could move back to Boston or NYC and pursue Theatre Arts, no problem. Even though I'd never been a professional in either of those cities, they felt easy, they felt like home. They felt like the natural, expected next step. Which is precisely why I turned the other direction!

Los Angeles, however, felt like a feral, confusing love affair that I was simultaneously terrified of and totally tantalized by. I was unconsciously conjuring my dance with the shadow, with my inner Kali, ready to blow my life up in the name of self-initiation. Thank Goddess I've come to realize since this time in my life that I don't always need to learn through crisis, that in fact, it does actually get to be easy. But I digress.

So, a few days before Christmas, I ripped the Bandaid and emailed Marie. I declared I was ready to give LA a go and see what the city had in store for me beyond a "semester at sea." She replied almost immediately that the PBS show she was currently producing was hiring. Now, she emphasized that she couldn't guarantee me a job, but she knew the hiring producer very well and would put in a good word for me with all the juju possible. Within days, I was on the phone with said producer being invited out to LA for an interview. And then it happened, that moment of vision when I could see, and also feel, my future unfolding before my eyes. That inner vision and sensation of knowing told me to book a one-way ticket to LA and not look back. It could not have been clearer. When you know, you know. Queen, TRUST IT.

Three weeks later, I walked off the KCET lot on Sunset Boulevard with my first professional job in television. For nearly 3 years, I had the privilege of working as the Traveling Outreach Coordinator for a bilingual talk show called "A Place of Our Own / Los Ninos en Su Casa." No, I was not standing in line with my headshot and pursuing my degree of acting, but instead, I experienced something far more enriching. I was afforded the opportunity to travel the country on the TV station's dime, and in the expansion of travel, I was also able to make an impact in local communities connecting local legislators with childcare providers who'd been highlighted on our show. This raised awareness at local and national levels on issues of early childhood education and development. It also brought me in contact with incredible women and their families, in unexpectedly intimate and powerful ways. To listen to their stories and celebrate their achievements I was being ushered into my sacred role as doula before I even knew what that was.

In this work, I also quickly began to understand the gift that studying theatre had given me; it was not to become an actress, it was to deepen my capacity for presence. It is through presence that healing is possible, and it was always the healing of the arts that kept me impassioned as an artist. As soon as my contract was over with the show, I knew my contract with LA was also over. I knew I was meant for a path of service, not a path of performance.

It's important to note that Los Angeles also proved to be my first descent into what we'd spiritually call a Dark Night of the Soul (i.e. a shit ton of shadow work). My job, and all the women who worked at that television station, literally saved my life. In LA, I experienced an abusive relationship and deep waves of loneliness and isolation. But I also witnessed my resurrection more times than I could count. Every time I leapt forward in self-trust, there were five other earth angels there to fortify that trust. Sometimes these were friends or co-workers, sometimes these were random yoga teachers in Santa Monica I never saw again. Sometimes these were twilight encounters with Coyotes in solo Griffith Park hikes. I kept moving in the direction of trust, and the world always made sure to send me a messenger of affirmation along the way.

In this self-trust, I've learned a great deal about risk-taking as a spiritual practice. I've also learned that I'm never asked to trust a vision for no reason. We are always being led by something larger, even if it doesn't "make sense" in the moment. This is the way of the Divine Feminine; the spiral path of life. When we act with trust, we understand that we're given everything we need one step at a time. No more, no less.

I could never have predicted what my life in LA would've been like, but I knew I had to go. In this rite of passage, I grew up. Or shall I say, I finally had space to grow into the woman I knew I came here to be.

Give yourself this space, Queen. Give yourself the gift of trusting yourself, even when it makes no sense, to you or anyone else. I guarantee it will lead you deeper to the core of who you really are, and when you hit that place inside enough times, you become unshakably, undeniably, unfuckably, YOU.

Truth + Self-Trust = bonafide Queendom.

And just to say, self-trust can be experienced and expressed as something very subtle. Grand gestures and leaps of faith are often topics of cool stories, but the daily listening to the subtle whispers and downloads of your intuition are what make for a fully grounded and embodied integration of this Sacrament. One foot in front of the other, just as Magdalene walked beside Jesus. Listening deeply in the heart of knowing.

Homecoming

"If a man does not keep pace with his companions,
perhaps it is because he hears a different drummer.
Let him step to the music which he hears, however
measured or far away."

- Henry David Thoreau

Death of the Martyr: The Why of Sacrament 6

I had a feeling come through me, a knowing that I was supposed to go visit my grandparents. Not just in that ephemeral "I should do that soon" sense, but in that very intuitively urgent sense of: *GO, NOW*.

My last day of work was on August 31st, and three days later on September 3rd, I was driving up the East Coast to be with them. On the surface, this urgency was rooted in the fact that my grandparents were in their 80's and 90's, and with Covid plus the impending winter flu season, I honestly didn't think I'd be "allowed" to visit them (not that I had Covid or the flu, but in that "good girl" precautionary way of being because they're at risk and I live a Wild Woman life). But underneath the fear of what could be in the future season, I had a deeper knowing.

My grandparents, particularly my grandmother, were dying. Frankly, as a three-time cancer survivor living on oxygen with COPD none of us knew how she was still physically with us in 2020 anyways. But to know my grandmother, Nancy, is to know the definition of warrior. This woman, born during the Great Depression, survived more trauma and atrocities than one person should have to, some we don't even fully know but simply speculate on as a family based on clues. A cat with 9 lives, to be sure.

One thing none of us had to speculate on, however, was that this was a woman who more fully embodied the definition of martyr than Webster could even begin to articulate in its dictionary. My grandmother, who grew up with nothing, was the epitome of giving. She constantly gave, so much so that I don't honestly think she even knew how to receive. Did any woman of her era know how? Were they ever truly allowed to know how? Perhaps it was just safer not to try.

Homecoming

Human beings are hardwired for resiliency, just as they are hardwired for connection. So, my grandmother found a covert way to receive: the receiving of genuine joy rooted in her giving, most notably through her exquisite baking and cooking (you have not lived until you have tasted a freshly baked raspberry or strawberry rhubarb pie from her oven). Her baking wasn't just on special occasions, her baking was a ritual act of service to all who crossed her path. Pies and cakes that could heal lifetimes of heartache or a belly full of teenage angst. In addition to desserts, she was an outstanding American cook. Every meal she prepared brought family and community together from far and wide. Never fancy, but always deeply nourishing. The more butter she used, the more belonging we felt. She created sweetness in a world that hadn't been sweet to her.

I spent every Summer in New Jersey with her and my grandfather, and every summer before my brother and I would make the 9 hour drive up the East Coast from North Carolina, my grandmother would call me and ask for any special requests. It was the same every time: raspberry pie. And every time, without fail, for 33 years, there would be a freshly baked raspberry pie awaiting my arrival. The last couple years of her life, she didn't have the physical strength to move about her kitchen, but the pies always got made anyway. They were made in her ritual phone calls (every Sunday morning, literally since the day I was born, this woman called), or the insanely generous checks sent on birthdays or holidays, or the abundant support during college or grad school, with care packages or an extra $100 to help me pay a bill. As a breast cancer survivor, it was she who sent me a check to help pay for my medical bills when going through my own breast lump journey. I could go on and on, but the point is she was a constant giving tree.

Because of her trauma history she wasn't necessarily that archetypal warm and fuzzy grandmother. She had a biting, sarcastic sense of humor that could instigate a fit of laughter in one sentence; together we could tell the world to fuck off, and when I was old enough, drink a glass of wine while we did! My grandmother was always there, in a way I only now realize that most of my peers can't conceive of. Growing up, I just always assumed everyone had amazing relationships with their grandparents the way I did. Growing up, I didn't know how rare it was to religiously have raspberry pies and big hugs waiting for me at every turn. I didn't actually know how rare she was until now.

See, I followed that knowing to drive up the East Coast to go visit her and my grandfather on September 3rd. Although I couldn't hug and kiss my grandmother because of Covid, I could be in the same room as her, so for 4 days I just sat with her.

She basically lived on her couch, unless someone was helping her use the bathroom or change clothing. Her short term memory had greatly deteriorated, and her hygiene and appetite had declined, as it does in those common stages of letting go before Spirit decides to leave the form. In this space, there really wasn't much I could talk to her about. She'd ask a question, I'd reply, she'd appear sharp as a tack, and then 10 minutes later we'd rinse and repeat. It was heartbreaking to realize in that moment that I had been called to visit, not to exchange ritual words or hugs, but to exchange presence. That on some energetic level, my grandmother might feel me as the Love in the room. "Be the love in the room," Elizabeth Gilbert often says. On this trip, I decided to be the love in the room by buying my grandmother freshly bloomed gladiolas. She loved flowers. I placed them on the mantle surrounded by endless pictures of all us grandkids, the ginks, as we were known.

As someone who grew up not having much of anything, the little things really were the big things to her. Perhaps this is why she had such a love affair with Hummingbirds, an animal whose spirit is deeply rooted in the frequency of JOY. In one direction, she could see the flowers I procured, and in the other direction, several humming-bird feeders on the deck to her right. From her perch, she could watch the sunrise and the sunset, the seasons flow through like seamless rites of passage, and take in the minutia of animal life passing by. I sat down across from her, after carefully placing the flowers on the mantle. There was a moment, a glance that seemed to say it all, an unspoken exchange from her to me: "That's enough, Sarah B." Not in the punitive sense, but in the expansive state of gratitude and awe that overcomes us as humans when we stand before the ocean and realize how small we are, or how we feel when we meet a newborn baby for the first time-the enoughness, the absolute understanding that simply being alive is the gift itself. My grandmother, me, and the flowers sat there for a moment just feeling that enoughness of being together, and it brought me great peace amidst the grief of watching her die.

The next day, as I was packing up to drive back down to North Carolina, I stopped in the living room to say goodbye to her. She scooted to the edge of her couch, so frail but still reaching for the connection. I remember welling up with tears and saying, "I'm so sorry, I wish I could hug and kiss you, but with this damn virus (Covid) they say it's better I not get too close since I've been travel-ing." She looked at me with the most confused eyes. Like, are you fucking kidding me?! So I knelt down as close as I could and just simply said, "I love you. I love you so much. Thank you for every-thing." And maybe that was enough.

Four weeks later, my dad called to tell me she passed away peacefully in her sleep, on that very couch.

As I drove back up the East Coast to go say goodbye to her body, I kept thinking how grateful I was for my own intuition that guided me to go say goodbye while she was still alive. Did I consciously know in September that she would pass just a month later on October 8th?

No, but that deeper part of me, that 6th sense, that 6th sacrament, knew. And I'm eternally grateful I decided to trust it.

Whoever you are, wherever you are reading this, may this be your permission slip to finally, without apologies, TRUST YOURSELF.

What your intuition guides you to do may not make "sense," in fact in my experience, it rarely does, at first. But also, in my experience, the larger wisdom at play is always revealed after the fact. What's required is that you act from this internal well of knowing; the "proof" that that action was "worth it" is revealed after the action is taken. This is faith. When we embody the 6th Sacrament of the Goddess, we are declaring, like the Joan of Arc in our own storyline, that we have faith, not just in life itself, but in ourselves. That we, too, just as much as anyone, are worthy of our own courageous, bold, decisive leaps towards love. It is loving to trust yourself. It is loving to trust life. It is loving to have faith in that which you cannot see but can unequivocally feel. This is the way of the feminine. This is the place of miracles. And we are all worthy of miracles.

Our trauma, our wounding, and our social programming will try, time and time again, to knock us off our axis of trust. It will force us into corners of disassociation and fierce self-protection. This makes sense. We are built to keep ourselves safe, and when that sense of safety is violated we respond in the most primal of ways through our fight, flight or freeze. But just as primal as these responses are, so too is the primal impulse towards Love.

In fact, to love and be loved, is *the* most primal force on the planet. So in moving from a deeper place of trust within ourselves and life, even when everything around us screams for us to do the opposite, we are participating in the most radical movement of our times: LOVE. When we are aligned with the frequency of LOVE, true love, we are aligned with the frequency of healing. We heal our cellular DNA, we bring healing to the spaces we inhabit, we bring healing to the hearts of those around us, we bring healing to the Earth grid we walk on, just by being alive and in LOVE.

To understand this as true, is to understand that your being alive is enough. The current paradigm of the last 2000 years benefits from our forgetting of this truth. This is why we have the Sacraments. They are rooted in our re-membering, and they are rooting for us.

The whispers, the downloads, the sudden flashes, the images, the gut feelings, the spontaneous emotional reactions, these are all facets of our intuition, and when we learn how to recognize them, listen to them, and trust them, we begin to create a world that's easier to trust.

There are tools you can use to access or practice these sacraments. There are rituals to release blockages getting in the way of your ability to embody them. But above and beyond all is always, and I mean always, your sovereign choice to choose it. Please remember that this choice can be easeful, and when it feels like it might be hard, go back to Sacrament 5 and Gather Your People; the people who really know and love you will always help you rise into the remembering of who you are and why you came here. It's a sacred contract rooted in Love, trust it ;)

Self-trust heals generations

My grandmother whispered something to me in a morning mediation a few days after her death. She said, "Sarah, I never got to be a woman. Not like you can, and are being. It wasn't safe for me to be embodied, let alone explore my sensuality, sexuality, or divinely feminine spirituality. I wasn't allowed to slow down or feel. So go do it! Be the woman I couldn't be. Go live your life! Who gives a shit what other people think. Just live your life."

It was my inner Feminine, my intuition that led me to drive up to see her one last time before she passed. So it will be my inner Feminine that honors her in the ways I live after she passed. She taught me to be hard-working and take action in my life (masculine), but now I get to bring her healing every time I practice the sacraments and choose to allow myself to slow down, honor my body, let my heart and intuition guide me, or embrace the mystery without apologies (feminine). It is bringing our whole lineage healing every time I allow myself to eat the raspberry pie, guilt free, and simply receive its sweet, sensual medicine for what it is, Love.

As we practice all the Sacraments of the Goddess, may we allow them to bless not just our own lives, but all the lives of the women who came before and those who will come after. May we trust that this healing is real and is happening. May we trust that this healing is *enough*. No over-giving required, just the honest, radiant *being* of who we truly are.

Practicing Sacrament 6
Overview

Shadow: A lack of openness to outside information that might support you. Rose colored glasses, illusion or delusion, paranoia.

Chakra: This Sacrament is connected to the 6th Chakra, located at the 3rd Eye. This chakra radiates the color indigo, that glorious hue between blue and purple. Physically, it is connected to the pituitary gland, located in the forehead between your eyes in your brow line.

This chakra is connected to our psychic faculties of vision and intuition. Seeing the unseen, or clairvoyance. This Chakra asks us to Trust what we see, even if it doesn't make sense to anyone else or even ourselves. We can trust what we receive in this chakra and this Sacrament because we know we've done the groundwork of the first 5 Sacraments to properly clear and align our physical and energetic bodies with our Soul's highest Truth, which is connected to the larger Truth of the Universe.

In this Chakra, our vision merges with the cosmic vision and we are led into the sacred co-creation of our dreams.

Earth Cycles

Moon phases: Trusting in oneself is an inner experience, as such, it is highly aligned with the energy of the New Moon. The New Moon phase is that dark womb, void like space where we turn our gaze inward and listen deeply for the visions, messages, intuitions, hits or downloads coming through us. We have to slow down long enough to see or perceive these messages, and as such, the 1st and 6th Sacrament are deeply connected.

On the new moon, take a moment to light a candle, close your eyes and turn inward. What are the life visions small, and large, you are working towards right now? What is your level of self-trust as you move about making these visions manifest? Where could you use greater trust?

Use the new moon as a time for reflection and visioning or refining your visions, so that you can actively take action during the time of the full moon to manifest or complete them. The new moon is simply a great time for prayer. Pray for the frequency of trust to come to you and work through you and see what wants to unfold.

Seasons: Trusting yourself is a 24/7, 365 kinda deal. There's never not a time where this is a good thing to practice or cultivate. However, I love approaching each new season with the inquiry of how can I exercise greater trust in myself? In the Fall, how can you trust what you're being guided to let go of? In the Winter, how can you trust the process of rest? In the Spring how can you trust the new life calling you? In the Summer, how can you trust the parts of you that are ready to shine and fully blossom?

Supports

Mantras:

- Choosing myself builds trust in myself.
- The Universe rewards the Trustworthy. The Universe chooses the self-chosen.
- My vision is clear and my intuition is aligned with Truth.
- I am the Joan of Arc of my own story.
- The more I choose me, the more I trust me.
- Just because others can't see it or feel it, doesn't mean it isn't real.
- I have nothing to prove. I am worthy of trusting myself.
- I receive clear guidance from the Universe through my inner sight. Visions guide me from within.
- I see and perceive clearly.
- My inner visions become manifest in the outer world through commitment to self-care and self-trust.

Divine Feminine allies:

- Athena
- Artemis or Diana
- Hecate
- Joan of Arc

Herbal ally:

- **Skullcap**: Skullcap calms our overactive minds and supports exploration of the subconscious so that we know what's running in the background. She clears out limiting

beliefs and strengthens intuition. Skullcap is the bridge between 99% belief in self and full-body Knowing.
- This herb can be ingested through teas, tinctures,and elixirs. However, simply meditating on this herb can bring powerful insight and awareness.

Songs:

- "Woman (Oh Mama)" by Joy Williams
- "Be Yourself" by Peruquois
- "Clairvoyer" by Random Rab
- "Antidote" by Yaima
- "Light of a Clear Blue Morning" The Wailin' Jennys
- "Priestess" by Pumarosa
- "Temples" by MC Yogi, East Forest

Integration tools:

Practice the first 5 Sacraments of the Goddess. Slowing down, especially, helps us to hear inner truth and guidance. In slowing down and honoring the body as a temple, we are often guided to a physical sensation or message that we are unmistakably led to trust.

Listening. Pay attention to recurring thoughts, ideas, and feelings. They have a message for you.

Embodiment. We learn how to trust ourselves by being with ourselves, so any kind of embodiment practice (including a simple walk around the block) will help us make contact with our intuition and knowing.

6th Chakra meditations. These are all about visualization. Find an app, youtube channel, spotify playlist, or any other tool you like to find guided meditations and visualizations. Sometimes simply taking your index finger and tapping on your 3rd eye can activate it and you can drop into your own self-guided meditation to receive visions.

Make a vision board or an altar. Create a physical representation of your visions to help manifest them into reality (see instructions in the elemental release and reclaim ceremony).

Purple, purple, purple! Eat, drink, wear or adorn yourself or your home with this color, as it activates your third eye center!

Muscle testing. Notice what you lean forward on, and go with it!

Remembering. It's really important to remind yourself of all the times in your life where you trusted yourself and things worked out because of it! It's also helpful to listen to other people's examples of this, as both will help bolster your faith and capacity for TRUST. We're human, we need to prove it to ourselves sometimes!

Invocations

Prayer:

Divine Mother, I call on you for clear vision within so that I might walk with clear alignment in my outer world. I ask you to fortify my Trust in Self as I take guided action based on these visions.

May I know that my visions don't have to make sense, that the way of the Feminine is wild and nonlinear, but inherently wise and loving.

May my visions bring healing to myself, my relationships, and the Earth.

May I see clearly, and may You help me to remove any fear blocking that clear sight. May I trust that it is safe for me to receive visions in this lifetime.

May I trust that my visions help birth the New Earth, one step at a time.

When all the world says it isn't possible, through Your Grace, may I know the impossible is made possible through clear sight, dedication, faith, and support when I need it. My visions move mountains. Your Love moves me into greater Trust.

I've done all I can do, there is nothing left but to Trust.

And so it is.

Journal prompts:

Self, Relationships, Earth

Homecoming

Sarah Grady, MA

Maiden, Mother, Crone

Homecoming

Free write

Elemental release and reclaim ceremony

This Sacrament is connected to the element of ether or space. This element can feel spacey and formless, no pun intended, so the below ritual is meant to ground you back into an embodied sensation of self-trust.

Creation of a dream board or altar: Making things with our hands grounds our visions into reality and supports our capacity to trust ourselves along the path of visioning. If making a dream/vision board, gather a piece of poster board or cardboard, your favorite magazines, scissors, tape/glue, and any fun decorative items such as glitter or googly eyes!

Light a candle, set sacred space, take 3-5 minutes to breathe and tune-in to your third eye. Ask to be shown a vision for any area of life where you're wanting change (e.g. new job, moving to a new city, calling in a new romantic partner). Make a mental note of the visions you are given and how they make your body feel. Then skim through the magazines, cutting out any images that relate to this vision and feeling. Make a sacred collage that externally represents your inner vision.

You can apply this same process to making a sacred altar. Altars are living, breathing spaces that hold the frequencies of our prayers and visions. We tend to them on a regular basis to keep the energy going. You can make an altar pretty much anywhere, with anything! I have a car altar on my dashboard with a few crystals and dried flowers to call in beauty and protection as I drive. I also have a floor-to-ceiling altar in my bedroom full of sacred objects, oracle cards, essential oils, and ancestral relics to support my prayers and intention for any given season.

Trust your inner vision to guide you in the creation of this. When you do, this altar will be a place you can come back to to fortify your trust. Sometimes just taking my first sips of coffee in the morning at my altar is all I need to fortify that self-trust, no prayers required!

Burn ceremony: I always suggest doing a burn ceremony for this sacrament. Throughout the history of patriarchy women have systematically been programmed to mistrust themselves, especially their psychic visions and intuitions. Hello, witch hunts!

So, conducting regular burn ceremonies to release any limiting beliefs or negative energy blocking your ability to trust yourself is highly recommended. Always remember to release, then forgive, then reclaim!! How does your body want to reclaim self-trust? Is there a place in nature that fortifies this? A relationship in your life that amplifies this? Is there a form of self-pleasure that helps you remember this feeling of trust. Let your vision guide you and go!

Sacrament 7:

Embrace the Mystery

Re-membering

There was a time when we weren't so afraid of the unknown. The mysterious, dark void space was the space of birth, of creation, of the miraculous.

We leaned into it with reverence and curiosity. We humbled ourselves before it, and waited patiently for it to reveal its signs and signals to us. We trained the inner eyes to see these messages and we trusted in the exquisitely perfect timing of their arrival and form.

There was a time when we weren't so afraid and life had a way of working out, and our rituals and ceremonies kept us in a faithful state of joy.

There was a time when it was even perhaps joyful to not know.

There was a time when we weren't so afraid because we knew Love would never leave.

Remember this time.

Embrace the Mystery

"What you are seeking is seeking you."

— Rumi

The beginning and the end

My love, you have come to the paradoxical Sacrament that is both the end and the beginning of your homecoming journey.

Most of us find our way to the Sacraments because the great mystery has stirred something in us that we can no longer ignore. A Soul-calling for change. We move through the first 6 Sacraments in order to come into vibrational alignment with that change in a way that honors our truest self: body, mind, and soul.

But just before that change can fully take shape, we must return to the mysterious force that stirred us in the first place. We must go into the darkness, stand naked before life, and LET GO. Let go of all we think we know about how or when our deepest desires will arrive. Let go of who we think we should be in order to receive them. Let go of any force or effort to manipulate our manifestation. Let go of any victim mentality blocking our birth, and instead lean in with the co-creative ear of listening, rooted in the heart.

We must become the ouroboros, the sacred symbol of the serpent eating itself, which symbolizes that cyclical nature of healing, the *internal* ascension of alchemy. In this sense, we return to the womb, the original home of all life, and allow life to birth through us, knowing we've done all we can do.

All that's left is to trust ourselves, and trust Life.

Trusting the nonlinear nature of life, despite how A-B we wish it was, is the ultimate embrace of the Feminine. When you welcome *Her* home, She brings *you* home in ways you couldn't have even dreamed of.

Get ready.

Remember, it gets to be good.

Mindset shifts that shift us

In order to truly embrace the mystery, there are some simple but profound mindset shifts that will propel you out of suffering and into deeper trust.

First, we allow ourselves to ***embrace* the mystery**, not try to solve it or hack our way through it. This can be quite confronting to the identity we may carry from being a powerful woman who gets shit done. That's OK, you're learning a new flavor of power, the flavor that understands the wisdom in the waiting. The wisdom in not needing to know everything all at once. The feminine wisdom of process over product.

To embrace something is to welcome it. Welcome to the waiting phase. You will soon begin to accept this necessary part of the process. You may even eventually begin to feel peace, joy, excitement, or relief in this place. Allow yourself to explore all the ways the mystery both terrifies and turns you on.

One key way of welcoming the mystery is to shift our thinking out of **scarcity and into abundance**. To do this, we accept that this is a vast Universe with more than enough resources for everyone. You have not, nor could ever be forgotten.

This belief is contrary to everything capitalism has taught us, but when you can truly allow the truth of abundance into your heart, you can then shift your thinking **out of judgment and into curiosity.** Creative solutions appear where before there were none.

Take stock of your life, notice how despite everything, all your needs have always been met. Everything always seems to work out. Maybe not the way you hoped they would, but they did. Equipped with this past proof, you can begin to notice the current of abundance working its way through your life in *this* now moment. Then, when someone or something shows up on the doorstep of your life in the future, particularly something triggering or uncomfortable, instead of judging it as bad or wrong, you can begin to open the door to it with curiosity. Then its arrival signifies a potential gift, not a punishment.

That gift might be an important lesson learned, a necessary healing, or the strengthening of your prayer itself. It's all a matter of perspective. No matter what the reason, when you make these subtle shifts in consciousness you begin to see life working *for* you, not against you.

In this way, we can see that the mystery is constantly offering us ways to grow.

Sometimes a particular life change requires more growth than others. My dear friend, Whitney, likes to call this being "cock blocked by the Universe!" It can feel like doors are closing everywhere. We can even internalize this to mean that we are doing something wrong. No, Luv, this growth period is not punishment, it is preparation for all the goodness that is trying to find its way to you. And it *is* trying to find its way. Like a diamond you are being buffed. No matter how long the labor, your birth is imminent.

If embracing the mystery is about trust, then we must understand the **technology of trust.** In order to trust anything there must be intimacy, and intimacy is built on vulnerability. Vulnerability is predicated on safety. So, Sacrament 7 invites us to get vulnerable with life. Lay it all out for Her; the good, bad and the ugly, your deepest fears and desires, no holds bar. Then watch Her perform miracles on your behalf.

In the experience of the miraculous, we begin to witness just how supported by life we are, and this creates an ever growing feedback loop of feeling safe in the world. Our sense of safety emboldens us to stay true to our path, continue taking leaps of faith, and embracing the mystery along the way.

The last mindset shift available to us in this Sacrament, then, is the *innerstanding* that the **mysterious *is* the miraculous.**

Patriarchy has trained us to be afraid of what we don't know. Let this sacrament entrain us to new neural pathways, seeking the miraculous in all we can't yet see. It's like being on a perpetual spiritual scavenger hunt. Eventually, you'll train your eyes and ears to perceive the miracles calling you. If you're not totally sure what that means, I invite you to ask life for billboard-level signs and signals that you cannot miss. Ask to be shown the missives that lead to your miracles. When you do, actively start to pay attention to the synchronicities populating your reality: everything from songs on the radio, to ads on social media, overhearing a conversation at the cafe that you needed to, or your friend reaching out about something you had just been thinking about.

Notice life speaking to you through symbols. Symbology includes numbers, colors, shapes, sacred images, earth elements, language and mythology or story. Embrace these symbols as messengers and sit with how they make you feel, what they may be trying to tell you, or invite them into your dreamworld. Eventually, the messages of the mystery will begin to reveal the answer to your prayers. You'll be guided to the right action step to take or how to recognize your dream come true when you least expect it.

Being on the spiritual scavenger hunt of life is about learning how to read between the lines of life. It's more fun that way, and it's definitely more Feminine. You'll begin to feel like you're in on a secret that no one else knows about.

There's nothing left to "do," but if you need something to do, let it be JOY: In a world where your value is predicated on your productivity, it can feel challenging to slow down and embrace the mystery; the reflex of doing is so strong in your system that to not do can feel deeply threatening.

Some people live for the permission slip of letting go and letting life work its magic. However, if you feel compelled to do something, or you're finding it hard to let go, you're not alone. The directive of this Sacrament, then, is to embody JOY. In other words, do whatever the fuck lights you up and makes you happy!

If you've taken action on whatever you're praying about, and you're now patiently (or not so patiently) waiting for life to answer you, this is the time to dance, make love to your beloved, tend your garden, swim in the ocean, read your favorite book, cook a glorious meal, call a friend, or anything that brings you genuine JOY.

Following your joy not only feels good, it is also the great distractor from our longing. When we are engaging in our joy, we are instantly pulled into the present moment. Staying in the present helps us release the grip of the past or future. In this way, we're no longer blocking the flow of life, but in fact, life is flowing through us.

Joy is also the technology through which life can find us. It's hard for the goodness we seek to find us when we're in a heavy state of depression, cynicism or anger. If like attracts like, then populating our life with joy is like sending out a giant flare into the sky so all the blessings can find us. Plus, people want to be around others who cultivate this sense of curiosity about the goodness of life. Yes, misery loves company, too. But ultimately, misery keeps us stuck, whereas joy expands us. Our expansion brings us out of the stuck places and back home into alignment. There is no sweeter joy than to celebrate this with others on the path. It reaffirms our whole purpose for being here.

Process not product

With joy as the directive of this sacrament, it can be somewhat misleading to think that embracing the mystery is a joyride. To be sure, there is an alchemical process at hand. You may not always get what you want, but you will always get what you need. In this way, there may be unexpected gifts along the way to your eventual stopping place. Be open to *receiving* them. Practicing Sacrament 1 can be really helpful during this phase. When we slow down, we can actually perceive the gifts we might've previously missed in the rush to get to the finish line.

Life works in mysterious ways. You may be connected to outrageously synchronistic people at just the right time. On the path to love, for example, your heart might get broken by the mystery in an effort to open it for the deeper love coming, which you need to be rooted in your self-worth to receive. On the path to love, the mystery might also bless you with really beautiful love that incrementally expands your capacity to receive the love of your life later down the road.

Not all learning must come through crisis. The mystery teaches us to be curious about the deeper meaning behind each part of our process, and how to savor it along the way without judging any of it as right or wrong.

Worth the wait

If the change you seek is taking longer than you hoped for, it's because something better than what you prayed for is on its way. The mystery of life always wants more for you than you do.

So just remember, if Sacrament 7 is the waiting phase, *you, dear Queen, are worth the wait.* No quick fixes or instant gratification will ever do for you, only the slow burn of the real.

You are the mystery

You cannot be defined. You cannot be reduced to spreadsheets and data points. To embrace the mystery is to embrace the most wild, vast, unclaimed parts of yourself and bring them home with as much curiosity and love as you can muster.

Be warned, though: the more you embrace your mysterious nature, the more others will try to define or categorize you in some way. This is in an effort to quell their discomfort with their own mysterious nature. It is not an invitation for you to rearrange yourself into something that makes more sense to them. When you feel yourself defensive or dumbing down, call-in Sacraments 3 and 5. Gathering your people to reinforce your "weird" will keep you steady on the path of homecoming. Don't you dare return to palatable people-pleasing. Life has so much more in store for you!

Some helpful reminders:

- When you find yourself frantically searching for answers remember: *If it were time to know, you would know.* This in-between space is when it's best to activate your joy.
- When you feel like you keep asking life for the same thing and nothing seems to be happening, make one genuine offering, then let go. Continually praying the same prayer signals your distrust in life. Life knows your prayer, so stop praying it and just LET GO.
- When it feels like everything is crumbling, remember, you are being cleansed. You are being emptied so the Universe can fill you with what's in higher alignment for your Soul.
- The mystery can feel confusing or painful at times. Do not bypass these feelings. Make ritual and ceremony out of them. Move them through you so you can find their medicine. Invoking joy is about balancing the medicine of grief, not erasing it.
- You are sovereign. Call the Mystery by any name you want: God/Goddess/Source/Creator/the Universe/Love/Orange juice, whatever floats your boat. As long as it feels supportive to you that is all that matters.
- You are not alone.

Personal Story:

Embracing the Mystery is the greatest investment in your wealth you'll ever make. The mysterious is the miraculous, and the miraculous is expansive proof of the abundant nature of the Universe.

Having lived in the most expensive cities in the country, I was used to the necessity of roommates to afford any kind of living situation. I went from city to city, roommate to roommate, straight to living with partners. I never knew what it felt like to have my own space, physically or energetically. No solo time to just dance naked or masturbate as loudly as I wanted. Tragic, for any Scorpio woman, I know. Until the mystery of life pointed me in a creative direction I hadn't previously considered.

When I moved from San Francisco to Asheville, I settled in with roommates for financial reasons. Cross-country moves aren't cheap. But as a 31 year old woman, no part of me actually wanted to censor my daily movements or tip-toe around others anymore.

The Universe heard my prayer loud and clear. One day, I got a message from a fellow Qoya teacher asking if I'd be willing to come pet-sit for her while she was on family vacation. She'd be willing to pay me, and I would have her house to myself. Tina had a cat that was basically a human temple priestess, named Serafina. So basically, this was a non-pet-sitting pet-sitting gig. Tina also lived in the equivalent of the Appalachian Ponderosa, custom built by her husband, of course, whose company blends architectural tenants of both Appalachian and Japanese influenced design. *Swoon.* Plus, Tina had a pole dancing pole installed in her basement for good measure.

Tina, are you fucking kidding me? OF COURSE I'LL COME PETSIT FOR YOU! I'll also lick your toes. What else do you need me to do???

I spent a week in Tina's house tending to sweet Serafina, but basically being in my own version of an Appalachian retreat center fantasy. Long, hot salt baths, followed by sexy pole dancing and wine. I wrote poetry on their front porch and watched shooting stars from their outdoor hot tub at night. If this was not abundance, I didn't know what was! At the end of the week, Tina asked if I'd ever be open to coming back, to which I attempted to play it cool with some sort of subtle, "Sure, anytime sister, so happy to support you." But let's be real here, Tina was full-on supporting me. Not just my bank account with a little extra spending money, but frankly my whole nervous system. Space, y'all. I finally had space... for *me*!

Unintentionally, one gig led to another, and within a few months I was regularly pet-sitting around Asheville, so much so that I was barely living in my own home with said roommate.

In a flash-moment, I understood what the Universe was trying to tell me: Girl, this is an abundant fucking world, founded on divine reciprocity. You are not excluded from that equation. The solution or answer to your prayers, though, might just look different than you anticipated, but they're always, and I mean always, delivered right on time, and with your best interests at heart.

In what felt like a come-to-Jesus moment, I saw a vision of me packing all my belongings up and putting them into storage.

No, I couldn't, I need a home!

... Or could I?

I mean, I'm basically wasting money every month on rent when I could pay less for a storage unit and try a cosmic experiment in the name of my Patron Saint! For those of you who don't know, Saint Sarah, or Sarah-la-Kali, as she's known by many, is the patron saint of the gypsies. Often known as "the dark one," she's the saint known for protecting the outsiders and outcasts of society, the gypsies and travelers of all kinds. My own inner black sheep, traveling-sprite-self always felt Her close.

And so, from Sacrament 6 to Sacrament 7 I leapt with trust, and a bit of fairy dust, into the mystery of full-time house- and pet-sitting. For nearly a year, I had no permanent residence. I put 1 notice out to the yoga center and community I worked in, but by and large everything spread word of mouth. For nearly a year, I moved all over the Asheville area having wild, beautiful, and abundant experiences. Often finding myself in ridiculous "You cannot make this shit up" moments that filled me with so much aliveness. I was expanded far beyond what my daily routine in a rental could've afforded me; this was straight up spiritual practice.

This time in my life, although nerve racking in some ways (as housing situations would often come through right at the last minute), always kept me in a perpetual state of gratitude, faith, and hope. Every time a new gig got offered, I felt more trust in life. It got to the point where I truly stopped worrying where I would be week to week and just let the mystery of it all guide and surprise me.

Now don't get me wrong, there were some wackadoodle people and quirky fucking animals, but that never outweighed the moments of joy or beauty.

I came to relate to this part of my life as a game, something to lean into with a sense of play, curiosity, and joy. In this way, I wasn't blocking life from supporting me, I was creating a clear path for abundance to find me.

I learned a lot about people in those days, the different ways people live and love and create a life. I got to try on all these different realities and feel for which aspects resonated and let go of the rest. It was a constant litmus test. It was the best speed dating, OK, *only* speed dating event I've ever participated in, and it was fun! It also provided the very necessary space for me to finally process the grief of having left an entire life behind on the West Coast. I embraced the mystery of gypsy life, and in turn the mystery embraced me with one giant abundant shoulder to lean on so I could finally feel it all.

My time in Asheville was one of healing. Some of the healing looked like the initiation of breast lumps, wondering if my body had cancer. Other initiations were of the love-life nature, falling in love with chronically unavailable Peter Pans, man buns and all. Other initiations were lightning bolt moments of creative or professional inspiration, doula and yoga teacher trainings (I mean, the 7 Sacraments of the Goddess were birthed in Asheville, after all!). Throughout each and every one of these milestones, I had the space to fully feel, fully process, and fully heal. To fully strip away all that I was too busy to look at in my hectic Bay Area life, but was finally ready to release in the arms of Appalachia.

Homecoming

This kind of pace is not for the faint of heart. We all need sacred pauses for integration. So, just as quickly as the mystery of life opened the portal of this experience, She began to close it. After a year, the gigs began to slow down, as did my love for Asheville. It was time to go. I received from those mountains what I had come for. Not necessarily what I wanted, but absolutely what I needed. Cue the Rolling Stones, "You Can't Always Get What You Want..."

I've come to find that if I'm willing to practice the first 6 Sacraments, by the time I reach the 7th on any particular life issue, I am given not just what I need, but more than that. Every time I surrender to life and embrace the mystery, I am met with the miracle of abundance. More love, more money, more opportunity, more adventure, more learning, more connection, more health, and more aliveness than I could possibly imagine. The first 6 Sacraments help me get out of my own egoic way so life can do what She needs to do. In this infinity loop of divine reciprocity, I give Her my trust, and in return, I always receive more reasons to trust.

I witness the immense privilege I've had in my life. I've never not had a roof over my head, food to eat, or clothes to wear. There were many moments on the path where I had no idea how I'd pay rent or put yet another grocery store run on my credit card, but even that is privilege. Sometimes I think my Soul planned it out this way. That I would allow my bank account to get so low or my love life to get so toxic so that I would have no other choice but to let it all go to something larger than me and just fucking free fall. The net has never not appeared, and in that, I've been bolstered to take more daring and courageous risks with each passing year. And maybe that's the whole fucking point.

I'm not perfect, and there are still things I long for, but at the end of the day, I can truly say I am happy. I can truly say I am alive. I watch seas of people stand on the sidelines of their own lives and place blame on everyone outside of them for their unhappiness. What I've learned from the Sacraments is that happiness isn't easy, nor comfortable. It's a continual choice. Some days this choice is much harder than others. But to wake up every day and recommit to this choice, which is an act of recommitting to yourself, builds a life from the inside out that is honest, true, sovereign. And perhaps that's why we feel so happy when we choose it, because we know that it was us all along that we were saving, and simultaneously seeking. And that the great mystery of life is simply handing us offerings in the direction of that choice every day.

May we be courageous enough to slow down and listen for these offerings, and then follow our body and heart's wisdom, without apology, to guide us, with love and trust, every abundant step of the way. Because what's the alternative? Well, let's just say you wouldn't be reading this book if the alternative was what you were still clinging to.

Queen, you're ready. You've been ready. Ready for the new way. Ready to remember and resurrect the old ways into your life today so you may never doubt your capacity to cultivate the life of your choosing again.

Congratulations! It's already done. It's already written in the stars, your only job is to embody these Sacraments on Earth so that which comes from the stars can come down to Earth. Talk it, walk it, allow it, and receive it.

Practicing Sacrament 7
Overview

Shadow: Being so open to life and surrendered that one never takes definitive action on anything, which can result in a lack of boundaries or out of control behavior.

"Oh I'll just let the Mystery decide or tell me what to do." No, Boo, a Queen consciously co-creates with the mystery, she takes action and then surrenders, it's not just full surrender. We're still living on planet earth! ;)

Conversely, a deep, unconscious need for control can take over and one can get lost in the mire of constant prayer, ritual, self-work and reflection without letting go.

Chakra: This Sacrament is connected to the 7th chakra, located at the crown or top of the head. Here we explore the realm of thoughts, wisdom, beliefs, and consciousness. This chakra is also thought to be our connection to divinity, spirit, God/Goddess, Source, Creator, whichever name you choose. It vibrates the color of Violet. However, when working with this chakra and Sacrament I often use the colors of black and white to symbolize a blank slate for co-creation with the Divine. It's totally your preference.

Working with this chakra supports a healthy relationship to the mystery of life, whatever words you use for that. When our crown is blocked we can become cynical and disconnected from life. We have the sense that we have to do it all on our own. Embracing the Mystery is about moving from self-trust into the trust of life, to know that we are always held in the watchful eye of the Divine. This is the chakra and sacrament of synchronicity, the language of the cosmos.

Earth Cycles

Moon phases & Seasons: The Great Mystery is all of life. She is every phase of the moon, She is every season and cycle. She is the ALL. She is everything, which includes YOU.

Use the lunar cycles to make prayers, offerings, intentions and plant seeds, but always, always take time to surrender those offerings, get still, breathe, and ask the Mystery to make Herself known to you. She might do this through animal messengers, a call from someone out of the blue, a synchronistic song coming on the radio that you haven't heard in years, or quite literally words written on a billboard, a message blasting straight to your heart from the highway. Trust it. You're not making it up. You're not crazy. Life has been listening to you, and now you're listening back. Every single one of these divine nudges fortifies you to keep going in the direction of your Soul.

Think of these messages like your cosmic cheerleading squad. Life becomes more fun when we're open to playing with it, so let every season and cycle be an opportunity for deep, cosmic play!

Note: every culture and tradition has a unique way of working with the Mystery. Take time to explore your biological roots to glean how your ancestors worked with the mystery. This is supportive to fostering a greater connection with your lineage, but also cuts down on the amount of cultural appropriation happening in the world. It's been a profound journey of grief, joy, and reclamation to learn about the Mystery from my Irish Celtic lineage. What rich history and practices exist for you, dear Queen?

Supports

Mantras:

- I believe in an abundant Universe.
- Divine timing is always conspiring on my behalf.
- Love lets go.
- The wisdom of every situation is always revealed to me in time.
- As I embrace the mystery, I move out of judgment and into curiosity.
- Curiosity is the conduit to the miraculous.
- The mysterious is the miraculous.
- I follow my joy, and life supports me.
- I'm being prepared, not punished.
- Life has not forgotten me. What I'm praying for has its own divine timeline.

Divine Feminine allies:

- Isis
- Ixchel
- Skuld
- Morrighan

Herbal ally:

- **Holy Basil**: The herb of divinity. Holy basil brings balance to our nervous, endocrine (hormonal), and immune systems and encourages deep spiritual healing from trauma. She connects all levels of body and being to Source.

Songs:

- "Synchronicity" by Rising Appalachia
- "A Change is Gonna Come" cover by Ledisi
- "Open" by Rhye
- "Dance Naked Under Palmtrees" by Mo'Horizons
- "Goddess Code" by Lizzy Jeff
- "Like a Prayer" by Madonaa
- "Authors of Forever" by Alicia Keys

Integration tools:

SURRENDER. Plain and simple, this is the Sacrament of releasing the illusion of control. However you practice surrender is perfect (prayer, ritual, being in Nature, etc.)

JOY! The most effective way to Embrace the Mystery, however, is to be in JOY! Anything that brings you joy and keeps you fulfilled in the present moment will accelerate the Mystery's communication with you. Plus, surrendering just *feels* better when you're embodying your joy instead of watching a pot boil! And the Sacraments of the Goddess are all about how we *feel* as we cultivate our ***Sacred, Sensual, Sovereign*** lives as **QUEENS**!

Invocations

Prayer:

Divine Mother, I bow before you. On hands and knees, heart open, mind humble.

I place my prayer on the altar of Life and let go. I fully surrender, I fully offer all that I cannot control to You. Help me to remember that the great Mystery is wildly abundant and always conspiring on my behalf.

Help me to move from judgment to curiosity.

Help me to know that the mysterious is the miraculous, and that I, just as much as anyone else, am worthy of a miracle.

I hand it all over to you, and in this renunciation, my heart and mind are filled with peace. I move forward in the frequency of Joy and allow You to meet that joy with an answered prayer in the highest and best way at the highest and best time.

And so it is. Thank you.

Journal prompts:

Self, Relationships, Earth

Homecoming

Sarah Grady, MA

Maiden, Mother, Crone

Homecoming

Free write

Elemental release and reclaim ceremony

This Sacrament is connected to all the elements: Earth, Fire, Air, Water and Ether. The Mystery is the ALL. So call in all the elements and see which ones want to work with you based on what you're moving through in life. Maybe you need more Earth for grounding? Or water for letting go?

When you've practiced the first 6 Sacraments and have exhausted and examined your current prayer in question from every angle, there's nothing left to do but LET GO. How does one let go or surrender? As mentioned before, engaging in anything that brings you JOY is a fast track to the Mystery working on your behalf. However, be careful not to bypass any feelings of grief, worry, doubt or despair in the process. To this end, I highly suggest a good ole fashion get-on-your-hands-and-knees tantrum!

As always, set sacred space. Light a candle, sit at your altar, go to a secluded nature spot where no one will interrupt you, or scream in your car in a parking lot! Let yourself be led to what feels right. Once in your proper place, choose whether you'd like music or silence, do a burn ceremony if need be, and if not, literally get on your hands and knees and just start speaking, screaming, crying, laughing, you name it! This is the snot-running-down-your-face moment where you have nothing to lose.

Go for it sister! Hand everything over to God/Goddess. Literally state "I let go, I give this to You know, please show me the way"

Once this ritual is complete, I suggest doing two things: drink your favorite beverage, and read the poem "She Let Go" by Rev. Safire

Homecoming

Rose. In fact, read it twice. This poem is my Holy Grail. When you read it, you'll understand.

Here's the deal: there is no right or wrong way to work with these sacraments. The prayers, mantras, music, herbal wisdom and rituals listed in this workbook are merely scratching the surface of what's possible. May they be the cosmic brainstorm to get your personal cosmic juices flowing, so you can embody yourself authentically, one Sacrament at a time.

Feel free to join me online in my courses, guided meditations, workshops and retreats for a deeper dive into all this work. But trust that literally all you have to do is say each of these Sacraments aloud, and they will guide you. They carry their own energy codes. They love supporting you in simple, sacred, sensual ways so your life of Sovereignty is truly your own. This is the way of the Queen: the physical embodiment of Goddess on Earth.

When we truly walk this path, our energy is infectious. Others can't help but want to join us. In this way we release the patriarchal standard of DOING and reclaim our right to BEING. Go be the Queen, crown yourself with no one else's permission, and the world will happily rise to meet you!

Beyond the Sacraments

We are All Works in Progress

By now you've figured out that the Sacramental life is not the perfect one, it's the honest and very often human one. Just because this work came through me does not mean I have it all figured out. There are many mistakes I've made, points of shame, and deep grief or longing. This is normal, this is good, this is human Queendom, too. I don't have it all figured out, but the Sacraments teach me every day that I am worthy of a seat at the table.

One such area of my life where I still have longing is in my deep prayer for sacred union with a man. For all the magic and success I've had in other areas of my life, this particular area has seemed to elude me. I'm not hard to love, so why has love been so hard to find? Maybe you know this question well, too?

I'm grateful to say that practicing the Sacraments has been the pathway to me unlocking the answer to that question; along with a recent practical, very real-world initiation. That straw that broke the camel's back moment. Oh, we tend to learn best through experience, after all, don't we?

Through this initiation, and midwifing myself through it with the Sacraments, I now know that it's simply a matter of divine timing before the vibrational match to my prayer is answered in manifest form. I know in my bones I've done all the work to strip away anything inside that would stand in the way of me receiving Love on the outside. And so it is.

But how did I get here? And why might this apply to you? Let me reverse engineer this for a moment.

Here we are, in the middle of a global pandemic. I'd already been through a couple of love initiations the last two years, and although neither of those experiences worked out, they did let me know that anything was possible. Like wild, men-dropping-into-my-reality, out-of-state, drive-15-hours-just-to-come-meet me kind of possible. Because that's what Kings do for Queens, right? ;)

The ongoing saga of my love life is quite literally a book in and of itself, but it was a moment back in November 2020 that wrote the beginning of the end of *that* book. Ironically, it started when I saw an ad pop up on Instagram for a new book. The author was a gorgeous man that was totally my type, who happened to live locally. I put attraction aside, however, because internally I felt that Spirit had placed his ad on my path to support my own book writing process. So I reached out. One thing led to another, messages were exchanged, and within 24 hours, I found myself on a coffee date with said gorgeous author.

From the moment we sat down together, IT. WAS. ON. This was not a book writing business meeting, this was a date in every sense of the word. I mean, I had NEVER met a man like this before. I'd certainly dreamed of him, but never had the blessing of a real world exchange. Not only was he physically gorgeous, but he appeared to be quite embodied, spiritual, articulate, intelligent, passionate, funny but also of depth. Everything in my body was shaking, it was an earthquake inside to feel that what I'd prayed for was real. It wasn't just in his self-expression that I felt myself leaning into, it was how exquisitely he held space for and acknowledged me, as well. He used language like, "I am aware that I am in the presence of an absolute Goddess." He also said something I'd never heard any man say to me before, "Just so you know, you are not too much. You are not too big. Not for me. In fact, I want to see you shine even brighter and get even bigger in the world. How can I support you in that, Sarah Grady?"

Are you fucking kidding me?! I feel like this is every conscious woman's wet dream. It was also my personal wet dream because I'd spent most of my life, even as a trained theatre actress, dimming my light and shrinking my body in order to fit in or make others feel more comfortable. Could it be that there was finally someone on the planet that simply loved me for me? Could I allow that and let it in?

And then it came, that Alanis Morissette "Ironic" moment. Go ahead, cue the song.

Almost two hours into this sacred coffee date, mister author decided to drop the bomb that he and his *partner* decided to move to North Carolina a few years ago.

Record scratch.

Wait what? Your partner?

It gets better. He then goes on to share that even though he and said partner technically dissolved their marriage a couple of years ago, they still lived together with their two young children and his mother in law. In addition to that, he had two other lovers, in two different countries. Why I didn't just get up from the table and never speak to him again, I don't know. Shock affects us all differently I guess. I was literally suckerpunched.

Let's back up for a second and talk about my track record for the unavailable. In my 35 years on the planet, I've dated gay men, trans-gendered men and women, the addicted, the traumatized, the finan-cially fucked and unemployed, the narcissistic, the mentally ill, the abusive, the sex addicted, the traveling musician-player, the polyamorous, and the married. Never was any of this information revealed up front. The pattern often looked like an innocent, cosmic encounter that felt trustworthy, to which I opened my heart and gave of it, and my womb, fully. Then, within weeks, months, or even years later a bomb would be dropped, and I'd be co-dependently entangled, trying to figure out how the fuck I got there... *again*. Like seriously, what the fuck did I have stamped on my forehead?

I'm a strong, articulate, well-educated and embodied woman. You don't meet me and think "Oh poor girl, she could really use some confidence." But clearly, I did need some, the kind of confidence that astutely sniffs out the unworthy and sets firm boundaries around them. That kind of confidence, however, is hard grown when your childhood survival skills are now stunting your healthy thriving skills as an adult.

A note on childhood trauma: common trauma responses or coping skills are to become hyper-vigilant, hyper-sensitive, and hyper self-reliant or independent. It is common for children of divorce or other trauma to be labeled as "so mature for their age," or become the parentified child. Society sees a young person filled with maturity and responsibility far beyond their years, but the child has develop-mentally skipped their own childhood in the attempt for self-protec-tion and preservation. It takes years to undo this behavior. If you recognize yourself in this, please be patient. Extend yourself, and the circumstances of your childhood forgiveness. You are worth the healing and liberation on the other side. Your healing and liberation are imminent. May the Sacraments, and the support of skilled practitioners, support you.

So, back to sexy author asshole for a moment. I wish I could say it ended right then and there at that coffee table, but it didn't. Although I thankfully never shared my body with this man, I was guided to share my heart for several more weeks. And now I know why. So it would *never* have to be broken like this again.

After weeks of daily deepened intimacy, filled with long voice memos and phone calls, I'll never forget the day it all came crashing down. I hopped on a FaceTime with him following a conversation he'd had with another lover, about me. He'd confessed to her that he loved me and wanted to be open with her about this. This did not sit well with her. In my experience, Polyamory rarely sits well when trust has been broken or the theory of what it means to openly relate meets the reality of human attachment. As he was describing her reaction to me being in his life, I began to get ill. I could taste the rage and the vomit rising inside me. This moment was all too familiar. I was now the "other woman." NO MORE. NO MORE. NO MORE OF THIS BULLSHIT!

For the next three days, he ghosted me while he chased after that woman, and I sat on the sidelines, holding space for all three of us. No one returning the favor for me. This was the lowest point. That moment when I had to look in the mirror and say, "Queen, when will you wake up to realize that you are worthy of so much more? It does not matter how cosmic of a connection this is. *This* is not Love."

Delivered by Love

It was Winter Solstice 2020, a legit birth canal for the collective consciousness, and I was midwifing my own birth. Ask any astrologer or empathic starseed about this day, and I guarantee you'll get a litany of similar stories. I practiced Sacraments 1-3 and unapologetically created space for my body and heart to slow down and really be with myself that night. To sit in the fire and let it all burn.

I went into full-on ceremony. On my hands and knees, I sobbed, I keened, I wailed, for what felt like hours. I had cramps in my womb even though I was weeks away from bleeding. I felt wave after wave of nausea and pain move through me until the birth of the Truth came out. And once it was revealed, there was no not knowing it. I had been delivered by myself and for myself, and this is what my baby told me:

My dearest Sarah, your core childhood wound in this lifetime is abandonment. It wasn't just that your parents got divorced, it was the chronic abandonment of self that you had to go through week in and week out to be a new version of you every time you switched homes. From age 7-18 you didn't know who you were allowed to be, and you didn't know which version of them you were going to get, either. Your imprint for love was one of abandonment. And in turn, you learned how to abandon yourself in exchange for the illusion of Love. Be a perfect little girl, be quiet, be nice, be a lady, don't cause a scene, don't speak up, don't be fresh, don't be too sensitive, in fact buck up and don't have any feelings, it'll just be easier for everyone that way.

Is it any wonder I found solace in the performing arts and literally got two degrees in how to master the art of becoming someone else?

And so, at the bottom of the birth canal, I understood that I had chronically attracted unavailable partners because if they were unavailable, then I couldn't truly be with them. And if we couldn't truly be together, then they couldn't abandon me. But *I* had to abandon me in order to be with them, just the way I'd done as a child over and over again. So my unconscious attraction to the unavailable partner meant they couldn't abandon me, but that also meant they would *never choose me.* And my whole life, all I've ever wanted was the soft landing of truly being loved for being myself. To be chosen as me, and to be loved in a way that actually honored me. An experience of truly being met, seen, attuned to and understood. An unconditional love, not a transactional one.

When I heard him say "You're not too big, you're not too much," I was seduced into believing that he was the one who had finally come to meet me on the bridge, the one who was finally here to choose me. We've all experienced this seduction. But as I lay sobbing on the floor, totally rendered, many supportive voice memos from my sister-friends later, I realized that no one would EVER choose me until I fully chose me. And no amount of self-betrayal would ever be worth the illusion of love. In fact, no amount of self-betrayal would ever be required for *actual love.*

What this man, and all the ones who came before, reflected back to me was my exquisite skill set of self-abandonment. *Not* my unlove-able-ness. I had co-dependently people-pleased and chameleoned my way into getting my needs met my whole fucking life. It worked, sort of, and I unconsciously thought that's what I had to do in Love, too. If I could convince the unavailable to become available for me, then I won. Childhood wounds healed, right? But that was never true. And this initiation helped deliver me to that Truth.

I am no longer a child trying to make sure mommy and daddy will continue to provide for my basic needs. I'm a sovereign Queen who knows how to provide for her own. As such, I'm clear that my prayer for partnership has nothing to do with being saved. I've already saved myself. Many times over.

My prayer for partnership is about the amplification of joy. It's about sharing the miracle of life with someone else in the most intimate and vulnerable of ways. It's about growth, learning and expansion. It's about play. It's about pleasure. It's about experiencing divine reciprocity. It's about shifting the human collective to higher states of consciousness right within my own bedroom. It's about knowing that I *can* do it all on my own, but that I don't *have* to. That I'm worthy of knowing the joy of being held just as much as I so fiercely hold others. It's about no longer apologizing for wanting to experience the fullest expression of this life and who I am in it. Not just the feminine or the masculine, within or without, but a true dance of union that makes the impossible possible.

I am worthy of this. You are worthy of this. Or any other prayer you hold deeply in your heart.

Just as Mary Oliver said in her poem, Wild Geese:

"You do not have to be good.

You do not have to walk on your knees

for a hundred miles through the desert repenting.

You only have to let the soft animal of your body love what it loves."

You my Queen are allowed to love what you love, and to be loved in return. No walking on your knees required.

Besides, Mary Magdalene didn't need Yeshua, but he sure as shit made her life more juicy, and their union made the world better because of it. So this is the prayer underneath the prayer. ***I pray for a Love union that makes not just my world better, but the whole world better. I am now fully ready to let that Love arrive.***

288

For sure you have proof in other areas of your life where choosing yourself has worked out. So don't you dare give up hope in an area where you are still in waiting. You are not being punished, Queen, you are being prepared.

I, and legions of other women, are standing hand in hand with you. So do your prep work, Sacraments 1-7 again, again and again. That which you wish for will come. It is law. Remember the reciprocal nature of the heart.

It will all make sense in the end, and if it doesn't make sense, then it's not the end. Keep fucking going.

You've got this, Queen. Your most sacred, sensual, and wholly sovereign life awaits. I can't wait to celebrate the arrival of your birth!

Marrying Myself

Remember that wedding dress from Sacrament 4? Well, that dress has played more of a cosmic role in my life than I ever imagined. In fact, that dress is what set into motion the writing of this book and the launching of my online school and women's center. Queens, everyone needs a dress like this. Or maybe a Sisterhood of the Traveling Pants but Sacred Priestess Queen style? Regardless, it's important to understand just how powerful we are and how quickly God/Goddess/Creator will move on our behalf once we declare our readiness for something. This book would not be complete without sharing this origin story.

It was October 2019 and I was packing for my upcoming pilgrimage to Ireland. Although many of my family members had already been back to our ancestral land, I always knew in my heart that my first, and perhaps all my journeys "home," would be solo. If you're a pilgrim, you know you need full spaciousness energetically to work with the grid of the Earth you're visiting, but also the Spirit of the people and the mythology of a place. As heroines of our open epic journey, we come to find that solo travel is the way our personal mythology has full spaciousness to get written.

And so it was that, for my 34th birthday, I was ready to re-write my ancestral narrative and open myself deeply to whatever healing, transformation, release or remembering was on the other side of that. So, I knew I had to pack "the dress," as it's famously known by my sister-friends. I felt that there was some sort of sacred ceremony I was to do in Ireland that would be both an offering to the land and my ancestors, as well as an offering to myself that could only be done there, on that soil, in that dress. It's a vibe.

As I was flying into the Dublin airport, I looked down to see the green, moist soil of my Motherland. Without any control, I just began to weep. In fact, I pretty much wept the entire time I was in Ireland. I wept tears of joy and love, tears of deep ancestral grief and loss, I wept tears of cleansing-a washing away of all that had been, so that I might be the bridge for my ancestors of what could now be. A moving prayer for safety, abundance, spiritual freedom, embodied freedom, and full expression of self without apology.

Although I spent most of my pilgrimage alone, I was blessed to stay a few days with a dear friend of mine, the saucy minx, Ms. Margarita Murphy. All this woman has to do is wink at you and you know a spell has been cast. Always in your favor, might I add. She's like my fairy godmother and my late-night-owl sex pillow talk best friend in one.

When I arrived at her home she asked, "Did you bring the dress?"

Homecoming

"Of course!" I giggled.

We began holding prayerful talk around when and where might be the perfect place in Ireland for me to slip on my second skin and go full priestess-style amongst the muggles.

Ironically, throughout my weeks of back and forth to the East and West Coasts, there was no such moment that got revealed. I had to go on the full journey first, embracing the mystery every step of the way.

And then, it came.

It was the eve of my last day in Ireland, and like a lightning bolt flash I got a strong pull to book a tour to Newgrange and the Hill of Tara. I'm a sacred solo pilgrim, group tours make me want to dry heave, but I knew I *had* to go. So, at 7 a.m. the next morning, I went traipsing through downtown Dublin, in full regalia, to get to the tour bus station. Local commuters gave me slightly lifted brows, but this is the country that literally diverts highway projects to protect fairy trees, so I think they saw me as kin. Who wouldn't want to drink their morning joe while wearing a priestess dress, right?!

I got on the tour bus, safely snuggled at the back where I had full spaciousness to begin the ceremony. I brought all my goodies with me: essential oils, oracle cards, herbal tinctures, copies of ancestral photos, and my journal.

I knew in my heart of hearts what today was. Today was my wedding day.

Was I ever going to marry another person in this dress? Who knows, and frankly, who cares? The most important declaration I could make to myself and to my ancestors was my readiness to fully marry myself.

Which is to say, fully choose, commit to, honor and cherish *me*. Because how could I ever expect anyone else to meet me on that bridge if I had not met myself? I'd been on a deep healing journey for decades, and it was time to honor that chapter so the next one could begin in full integrity and love.

The tour bus guide was a charming Irish man, who was frankly bashful around me in my second skin. At one point, he leaned over and whispered to me, "You know you are an embodiment of the Bridget, right? You are the Goddess." This felt like a divine nudge. I was right on time, with Earth Angels to prove it.

In the back of the bus I furiously wrote my wedding vows to myself. My hand almost couldn't write fast enough. All the vows I was ready to make again and again in the name of true self-love.

As we approached Newgrange, an ancient site older than the pyramids of Egypt, I had full-bodied chills. This site is very much a womb; you enter in a long, narrow canal as you would a vagina, which then opens up into an earth covered dome, full of ancient fertility.

One of the last tour participants to leave the space, I heard the Goddess whisper to me, "It's time now. You don't need anyone to witness you. Just go find a spot outside of this womb to plant your bare feet on the Earth and make your vows." Obedient, I found a stone gathering to the left of the entrance. I waited until other tourists had passed, slowly took off my shoes, put all my belongings down and went to retrieve my journal. I opened to the page where I had written my vows, and almost as quickly as I opened it, a force beyond my control closed it and flew it down to the ground.

"Sarah, let go of all you have written and just BE HERE NOW. Trust us, we've got you."

Homecoming

In that moment, the sun rose into the sky right above me and began to pierce my face, my heart, and my womb. Just as oceans of tears flowed from me upon arrival to the soil of Ireland, they began to flow again. I was naked, I was rendered, I was ready.

And so it began.

Like a sacred prompting, I felt the Goddess Bridget, I felt Danu, I felt my ancestors, I felt the Earth, and I felt my Soul and all the lifetimes she'd ever been in bondage all of sudden breaking free, I felt all of those energies say, "What do you *really* vow?"

Right then and there, I vowed, just like the sun piercing my body, to shine as brightly as I could. No holding back. Ever. From this day forward I would shine unapologetically for the world to see. That my light might be a healing not just for myself or my family, but be a giant permission slip for all women everywhere to shine their light too. A collective liberation of women.

I vowed to let go of anything standing in the way of me being this light in the world, any belief, any relationship, any addiction, behavior, pattern, job or experience that would block me from knowing and expressing the full Truth of who I really am. I vowed to fully embody and teach the 7 Sacraments of the Goddess for the rest of my life. To do my part in shifting the human collective into higher states of consciousness. I vowed to help the collective to remember how to Love and be Love. I vowed to always follow the physical sensation of truth in my body and honor my body's messages and knowings. I vowed to let my heart lead, and to allow my mind to be in service to the heart. I vowed to ask for support when I needed it. I vowed to let go of and forgive all the times I'd betrayed myself so that I could now walk with an unshakable sense of self-trust. I vowed to understand that in embodying the light so fiercely, I would be met with equal shadow, but to trust that this was natural, and that I was always safe and protected. I just kept vowing to shine as brightly as I possibly could. No more hiding. Ever again.

What started as a solo ceremony turned into several bystanders taking photos of me and standing in awe. No one stepped in, no one asked questions. They all seemed to understand the necessity and the sanctity of what was taking place.

As I felt the wink from my energetic witnesses signifying that my ceremony was complete, I felt 200 pounds lighter. I felt ages younger. I felt reborn. I knew something massive had just happened, but I didn't want to get my mind involved yet. I just allowed myself to feel it. It felt a bit like walking on air.

I also noticed a Japanese couple staring and pointing at me. Turns out, they had been on the tour bus with me the whole time. When we transitioned from Newgrange to another historic site, the Hill of Tara (complete with the famous Stone of Destiny which, yes, looks like one giant penis emerging from the ground) I was approached by this couple. Sheepishly they giggled and came up to ask if they could take a picture. I assumed they meant a picture of themselves where I had been standing, but no. Of me. They wanted a picture just of me. The wife came up beside me and said, "You Venus, aren't you? You the Goddess Venus, or Aphrodite, here on Earth. You came." I assured her I was simply human, but knew what she meant. Very much so. My light had, in fact, been turned on. All the way up, full voltage for everyone to see.

I took that moment to reflect back to them the beauty I saw in them as a young couple and blessed up their love. The next day I began my journey back to the States. I knew I was not returning home as Sarah. I was returning home as me, more fully than I'd ever been, whatever name that was called.

Homecoming

Almost four months later to the day, the planet was initiated into a global pandemic and full fledged lockdown brought everything to a screeching halt. Not only had my life as I'd known it been released to the fires for something new to emerge, but now the entire planet was in the same sacred descent.

At a time when most people were unexpectedly finding themselves isolated and on the unemployment line, I was blessed to maintain my work with one client and her baby boy. Not only were we support life-lines to each other at this time, but it became evident that in exchange for me caring for this woman's child, I was receiving daily support in stepping up into my light.

The 7 Sacraments of the Goddess and Homecoming were being born, as I was supporting the postpartum birth of this baby boy. Every day, Melea would talk to me about my vision and how to get it off the ground. She believed in me more than I believed in myself at times. She was there to reflect back my fiery Irish light every day, until I knew in my bones there was no going back on the vows I'd set into motion at Newgrange. No hiding behind my doula work or any other facet of my life that was not a holy hell yes! Within a very short time, everything else began to fall into place. Without much effort on my part, the Universe provided a business mentor, a book writing coach, income and spaciousness to begin writing my book and eventually devote myself to it full-time. I connected with amazing women locally, and around the world, who were desperately needing the kind of work I had to offer during this time. And so it was that in less than a year, my online school got launched, and this book got written.

I remember when Mary Magdalene downloaded the Sacraments to me. I remember when she adamantly told me I could not immediately teach them, but had to go out and live them. I remember Her saying in no uncertain terms that She would let me know when it was time to birth this work publicly in the world. My wedding day was the day I declared my readiness to Her, and the advent of Covid-19 was when She declared the world's readiness for me. For the Sacraments. For a better way. For the birth of the New Earth, one Queen and King at a time. My life, the living testimony.

May this story, and all the stories of this book, be divine nudges to your Soul to just fucking GO FOR IT. Whatever it is. The thing that you and no one else came here to embody on this planet. Whether it is a creative endeavor, growing a garden, birthing a baby, or quitting an addiction, trust it. For the love of all that is holy, trust the urgings of your Soul, strong and subtle. And when it doesn't seem clear or even possible to accomplish, remember the Sacraments. Slowing down will always create a foundation for success. When we show up fully for life, we give life the opportunity to return the favor.

This does not mean it is easy. In fact, the path of the spiritually conscious initiate is often the harder path. On this path, we sign up to feel, process, embody, and create things that not everyone has the courage to do. The joy and freedom that awaits us on the other side, though, is always worth it.

Follow your joy, gather your people to fortify your endurance, and remember, none of this happens over night. This roadmap of the Sacraments is a daily re-commitment, and in that we are held not to a standard of perfection, but to our self-appointed gift of permission. A daily crowning. There's no way you can do this wrong, and it's never too late. It is simply Love in motion. I love you. You are loved. Always, and in all ways.

In Sacred Service,

Sarah Bryanne Rose Grady.

P.S. Rose is my Confirmation name. Confirmation is one of the 7 Catholic Sacraments. Even in my early teens I could feel the Rose lineage of the Magdalene and all the Mary's beckoning me. Oh how the Mystery brought me home all these years later!

Homecoming
There's Room for Me

Although the book of the Sacraments began energetically writing itself in 2017 following my initial visitation from the Marys, it was a life-changing trip to Savannah, GA in May of 2020 when the transmission began to take physical form. Savannah, Herself, felt like a warm, mysterious womb that I never wanted to leave. She called me back to her waters every 6 weeks for a year until I couldn't help but move here. Savannah has been my mystical muse, a creative poultice of sorts, pulling forth sacramental transmissions from the moment I arrived. What I wasn't prepared for, however, was what She would personally give me in return for saying yes to birthing something for the collective.

Nearing completion of this book, I moved into my own home. The first and only home I've ever lived in by myself.

As a healing artist, drawn to live in beautiful (and therefore expensive) places, I've always needed to live in shared or borrowed space in order to afford life. It's never what my body wanted, but what my bank account could afford. Sound like a familiar bargain?

Savannah, however, made space for me to make something else possible.

I've always created sacred space wherever I went, building altars on my childhood dressers before I even knew what an altar was. It is something quite different, however, to land in a sacred space of one's own, unpack and stay awhile. The process of rooting shifts something on a cellular level of our being that cannot be articulated, only felt. And feeling is how the Divine Feminine operates at Her finest.

I sat down at my altar—candles lit, heart open—listening for any last transmissions from Source that needed to be included in this book. I received the words of "remembering" for each Sacrament, and then I heard Magdalene and Jesus whisper to me, "Go deeper, go into cere-mony, Sarah."

We cannot say for sure, but it is postulated that Sarah is the daughter of Mary Magdalene and Jesus. Whether there'll ever be factual evidence of this or not, I can say that in that moment, it felt like the parents I never knew lovingly guiding me to a sacred threshold. I knew what they meant by "sarah-mony."

"Ceremony," for me, usually means sacred self-pleasure. Just as the priestesses of ancient Egyptian, Sumerian, Indian, and Greek temples would perform sexual rites of passage for healing, I, too, alchemize, heal, and learn through the portal of pleasure. I dedicate my orgasms to something larger than me. I allow them to move me into states of higher consciousness. When I cum, I come closer to God. Antithetical to modern day Christian teachings, to be sure, but rooted in the Truth of the Magdalene-Christ path pre-patriarchy. This is where I am most at home. This space is my deepest space of re-membering. And so, it is no surprise that as I neared completion on this book, my spiritual parents wanted to send me two final care-packages that my body and soul would never forget before fully rooting into my new reality.

Lying on my bed, team of spirit guides and teachers as my witnesses, I began to writhe in pleasure. Stroking my clitoris with an obsidian yoni egg, blessed by the Grandmothers of Moon Dance in Mexico, I asked to receive any insights, healings, or messages that were required for me or the book. As I was edging closer and closer to climax, I began to notice how loud I was getting. I've been known to be quite vocal in bed prior to this, but this was different. Something deeper, something primal was erupting from within me. I was screaming in ecstasy so loudly I thought for sure my new neighbors would be calling the cops to ensure my safety, or sanity. By the grace of the Goddess, no such thing occurred. Instead, I experienced one of the most profound orgasms of my life. I was above it, witnessing it as it was happening, and then it hit me like a ton of bricks: I was scream-ing, crying, and expressing myself more loudly than I ever had because there was ***finally space*** for me to do so.

For the first time in 35 years, I was in my own space. 35 years of contracting, holding in, and energetically tip-toeing around others got completely dismantled in one orgasm. As both a doula and a shamanic energy healer, I'm well acquainted with the process of birth. This ceremony was truly a self-assisted re-birth. On each exhale of my orgasm, I began to see my entire life flash before me. I saw myself come out of my mother's womb, and I saw every person, place, and situation in my life where there had not been room for the totality of me. Every moment where I had made myself smaller to fit in, belong, stay safe, keep the peace, or make money; every time I had bypassed my own knowing in order to please others.

I saw so clearly all the cages my Soul had put me in so I would know the art of breaking barriers. I saw so clearly that I had to know what it felt like to stay small, so that there'd be no other option than to boldly

301

move in the direction of my bigness-no matter how much that terrified the parts of me that just wanted to experience the illusion of safety that a cage offers. Isn't that what we all want? Safety, security.

But I've come to understand and embody that the only true security we have is being in alignment with our Soul. When we are, we walk the Earth with an integrity, a clarity, and a self-love that is very hard to control. We must seek the spaces, within and without, where there is room for us. And if we find those spaces hard to find, we must carve out our own.

A fully inhabited woman is a woman who is home. When we're living life from that internal sense of belonging, we need not search for it outside ourselves. When a woman finally has space to inhabit the full space of herself, everything, and I mean *everything* about her and around her changes. She starts asking for more, and knows her worthiness of receiving more. She also gives more of her true self, not her co-dependent, people-pleasing self. In this way, she begins to experience true divine reciprocity. When a woman is received by others for the totality of who she is, this creates a feedback loop of neural pathways that emboldens her to take risks, stand up, advocate, and create fiercely in the name of Love. She shines brightly, and gives others the permission to do the same. She glows differently. She feels fed by life and in turn nourishes the life around her deeply. She understands the technology of the heart as the pathway to true abundance, which has nothing to do with money. But also, she understands that she's worthy of money energy to support her being who she came here to be.

Every job, every industry, every relationship, every city, and every family dynamic where there wasn't room for me in the past were gifts pointing me in the direction of where I stand now. Because I didn't settle for a life of squeezing myself in somewhere, I now get to experience the expansion and the true health that comes along with being here now. In my body, in Savannah, doing the work I was put on the planet to do. This has not been an easy path, but it has been honest and the only one I could've taken.

I pray you find your space, too. Whether this is a physical place, a sacred relationship, or a craft that makes you feel like you're flying, you will know it when you feel it. I pray you follow the feeling. I can't promise you that all the feelings along the way will be rainbows and unicorns, but I can promise you that if you follow them, they will lead you deeper and deeper back to yourself. They will bring you home.

We Made It

About a month into my new life in Savannah, I signed up for a swanky yoga + dinner event at a local historic Inn. Not because I had any business spending an extra $100 on myself, but I had a felt sense I was supposed to go.

If you take only one thing away from this book, let it be this: listen to those internal nudges. You are not crazy, you are being given divine guidance. Trust it.

There were four class dates to choose from, so as per Sacrament 2, I muscle tested my body to feel for which one would be most generative for me to attend. My mind wanted to attend one, but instead my body kept telling me to sign up for a different date.

When I get such a strong message in my body, I'm obedient (and then I usually go listen to the Rolling Stones "You Can't Always Get What You Want" when I have angsty feelings about said messages received!).

Go ahead and roll your eyes at the first-world problem of choosing the right date to attend a fancy yoga event, but I am forever grateful I listened to my body, because it set off a chain of events I truly could not have predicted.

After a luscious yoga practice, I got seated at a dinner table next to a woman named Kara, with whom I instantly hit it off. It was like a 6 degrees of separation with Kevin Bacon moment when we realized we'd gone to the same grad school in San Francisco, amongst several other synchronicities. We exchanged numbers, and I left feeling grateful for a new friend.

But that's not where this ended.

Several days later, Kara texted me to ask if I did pet sitting, and if so, would I be available to come watch her cats in a few weeks.

Did I do pet sitting? Cue a reading from Sacrament 7!

When I said yes, she invited me over to have lunch so I could meet her wife and kitties, and get acquainted with the house.

For those of you who don't know, Savannah, GA is one of the most Irish cities in America. In fact, it boasts the largest St Patrick's Day parade outside of NYC. A huge portion of Savannah's population claim Irish ancestry, and I find that this ancestral tie plays a significant factor in why and how I ended up in Savannah in the first place. But that's for another book.

It's also important to note that my paternal grandfather's name is William Grady. His side of the family, who immigrated from Ireland, are buried in a Vermont cemetery under the Tully headstone. My grandfather and I made annual Summer pilgrimages to visit the Tully-Grady ancestors, and it was these trips that began my fascination with ancestral healing.

Homecoming

I walked up the steps to Kara's home and noticed a historic placard, common to locally restored homes in the area. When I looked at the placard more closely I noticed that it read, "Built for William Grady and Barnard Tully in 1871."

If that wasn't missive enough, Kara's wife opened the door to greet me and began asking my story of how I got to Savannah. Because I've moved a lot in my life, I always start at the beginning: being born in New Jersey, of course! Immediately, Kate asked me where in New Jersey. I said, Montclair.

With a fairy-like grin on her face she asked, "Any chance you know a place called Tierney's Tavern?"

My jaw dropped. Tierney's Tavern is the local watering hole in Montclair that my maternal lineage has been patronizing for generations. In fact, it's still customary for my cousins to visit Tierney's after work or to celebrate life's milestones. Almost every family story on my mother's line starts with a nod to Tierney's.

Kate then revealed her last name. "I'm Kate Tierney, my great-uncle and his brother were the original owners of Tierney's."

Of course. You cannot make this shit up.

Standing in a home embodying the intersection of my maternal and paternal ancestral lineages, I was awestruck at the divine orchestration of my life. All because I decided to go to a yoga class. All because I listened to my body.

Two weeks later, I arrived on the same doorsteps to officially pet sit. To know Savannah is to know that this is a city of bathtubs. Almost every home comes outfitted with a ridiculous clawfoot tub or a modern day version of the like. To know me is to know that I am most at home in the water. So naturally, the first thing I did upon arrival was draw myself a bath. It would've been enough to simply indulge in the beauty of this moment, to literally soak in the blessing of warm water in a beautiful home with beautiful new friends. But then my body started to speak. It was time for ceremony.

This kind of ceremony was not a sacred sexual one, but it was a re-birth of sorts. I was guided to submerge my head under water, something I'd not done in months. It felt healing to hold my breath and just be beneath the surface. A true sensation of being back in the womb. When I reached the threshold of needing to come up for air, I gasped. I couldn't stop gasping for air.

I looked around the bathroom to try and ground myself and all that would come out of my mouth was, "I'm home. I'm home. I'm home," like a mantra being chanted in the holiest of temples.

Then my gasping and chanting erupted into sobbing as something else took over and the only words to come out of my mouth then were, "We made it." I placed hands on my heart, and like rocking a baby back and forth, I rocked myself for over an hour to the words, "We made it."

Knowing that an energetic portal had clearly been opened up, I, Sarah, started to ask, "Who is we?" Was this a soul retrieval? And was little Sarah now home with my adult self, my soul self?

"No," they whispered, "look around, look where you are." In a home built for William Grady, owned by a member of the Tierney family from NJ, in the Irish city of Savannah, GA "WE" meant my ancestors. "Because you're alive, in a body, living exactly where you're supposed to be, doing exactly what you're supposed to be doing, free, we made it. We can rest now. You're home sweet girl. You're home."

Homecoming

And then I understood in a flash what Homecoming really means, and how the 7 Sacraments of the Goddess are my Soul's roadmap to get there. Homecoming is really the process of letting go of all that isn't home so you can fully embrace everything that is.

We must go outside ourselves and do the necessary and messy work of trying on all the inherited programs, beliefs, and patterns of our family or society; and all the identities, behaviors and places associated with those. We must dive into the shadow of external expectations and "forget" who we are in such a way that our wholly/holy unsustainable discomfort has no choice but to lead us right to the threshold of re-membering.

We think home is a safe final destination outside ourselves to rest our bones and be. But the process of homecoming reminds us that true home is inside us, and is us.

Home is the river of essence that flows through us across all time and space. The ineffable and unseen energy that makes you *you*.

We take on jobs, relationships and identities that we think will make us feel that thing inside. It is the opposite. When we finally slow down long enough to be intimate with who we really are, unapologetically, then and only then can other people and situations that truly mirror back that essence begin to populate our lives.

When we meet a beloved, or travel to a new city and proclaim "This feels like home," what we really mean is: "The essence in them is simply reflecting back the true essence of me, and in this sacred mirror I feel safe, I feel seen, I feel alive, I feel a little less alone."

This energetic exchange creates a sense of belonging, but to be clear, there is never not belonging, only your choice to choose it. So, with every breath and every Sacrament, you are choosing a sacred belonging to self that can't help but attract an external world which enthusiastically joins you on the river.

My "poor Irish slob" ancestors, as they were often called, didn't have the luxury of living a soul-based life of homecoming, they were just doing their best to survive. And because they did, I'm alive to rewrite a new story. Which is this: we are worthy of more than mere survival. We are worthy of thriving.

Old structures are falling, and in their place we are birthing a new Earth, one that looks a lot like the ancient one. An Earth where not only is our Soul welcome as the driver of our experience, but is, in fact, required.

In this New Earth, there is room for all of us, and my tale of landing in the Grady-Tully house of Savannah will no longer be seen as a magical moment of kismet, but instead, a commonplace byproduct of people who know how to find home from within. They'll know how to find it because they'll never be told they have to leave it in order to belong.

We are in the birth canal. Hold on to the sacraments through each contraction. But don't doubt for a second that birth is imminent.

As humans, we may suffer grief and loss from time to time. This may trigger old fears and wounds of homelessness. This is natural. Welcome your shadow to come dance with you and inform you. Then call in the Sacraments to help row you back to the river.

The goal is not to be unaffected by life, the prayer is to allow yourself to feel it all, and to remember your resiliency.

Closing Prayer

In that still place of the heart where lovers meet, I invite you to meet yourself.

Slow down, take a breath, and when you're ready, recite this prayer.

This prayer is, in fact, your sacred marriage vows to yourself, dear Queen. These vows are your daily re-commitment to yourself, first and foremost. They are a reclamation of what is already yours, your divine inheritance. Say them as often as you need or want, for when we commit to ourselves, we belong to ourselves. When we belong to ourselves, we find belonging in the world. And with belonging comes great FREEDOM.

True liberation is the remembering that we are already born free. We need simply exercise choice to choose this freedom. And when one woman chooses it, she liberates all women around her to choose the same, in ways grandiose, and sacredly subtle.

<u>This we pray:</u>

I, (insert name), vow to Slow Down, Honor My Body as a Temple, Not Apologize, follow my Heart Compass, Gather My People, Above All Else, Trust Myself, and Embrace the Mystery.

I vow to shine as brightly as I can,

so that my light might give permission for others to do the same.

I vow to be kind to my body and others' bodies.

I vow to listen to the infinite wisdom of my heart.

I vow to remember I'm worthy of support,

and I vow to allow myself to receive that support.

I vow to remember that Queens don't compete, they celebrate.

I vow to uplift those around me, knowing that when I rise, they rise,

and this brings healing to the entire planet.

I vow to walk in profound gratitude and reverence for Mother Earth,

for She provides for my every need.

I vow to prioritize my pleasure.

I vow to take up space.

I vow to use my voice.

I vow to listen.

I vow to follow my joy.

I vow to release perfection and give myself permission

Homecoming

I vow to be the Love in the room.

I vow to remember that the mysterious is the miraculous.

I vow to move from judgment to curiosity.

I vow to trust myself.

I vow to remember that this is an abundant Universe that wants nothing more than to see me, and all beings, thrive.

I vow to remember that I am good enough.

I always have been, and always will be.

I vow to release any guilt, shame, worry, martyrdom, or doubt standing in the way of me knowing this Truth, allowing this Truth, and walking this Truth:

IT GETS TO BE GOOD.

RIGHT

NOW.

TODAY.

THIS MOMENT.

THIS BREATH.

FOREVER AND ALWAYS.

And whenever I forget how to align with that Universal goodness, also known as Love, I call-in the 7 Sacraments of the Goddess and I let them lead me back home.

And so it is.

It is so.

It is done.

The Final Re-Membering
The Codes

There is a voice within you

that will never fail you.

It is uniquely your own,

connected to your Soul's blueprint

but is also connected to the Universal voice that governs all,

the voice of

Love.

To hear this voice you must turn

INWARD.

We have been programmed for the opposite,

OUT,

and yet notice

how many times this voice,

your loving Soul voice,

has saved you and guided you

Anyway.

This is the power of

LOVE.

The codes embedded within this voice

want you to know that your

suffering is

NOT required

(and no longer welcome)

We are at a great tipping point on the planet Earth.

Your physical body is your personal planet Earth.

The codes of Love embedded in your DNA are asking for your attention.

Imagine if you were just as diligent

focused

aware of

hypervigilant

and protective of

your joy,

peace,

health,

healing and

PLEASURE

as you were your suffering or trauma.

Honey isn't lazy or selfish

Honey is sweet, nourishing, healing, and

PLEASURABLE.

Honey is also the by-product of extremely diligent work and effort

of thousands of bees working individually and communally towards a common goal.

In the quantum field of reality, what we observe or focus on grows,

what we observe becomes reality,

If we choose to only observe that which causes suffering,

we stay in suffering.

The Codes of Love

ask that you not ignore what causes the suffering,

just as bees don't stop working and pray honey miraculously appears.

The codes embedded in your DNA are intelligently engineered for RESILIENCY.

Which means this:

Do the work of GRIEVING.

Actively grieving creates a portal of alchemy

grieving allows for the acknowledgement of pain without bypassing it

AND creates space for the pain

to MOVE, to transform, and transmute

into something more useful,

something

healing.

For this reason,

you will find that many indigenous cultures around the world actively grieve through rituals that are also infused with

JOY.

When you place your grief on the altar of life

and use the technology of dance, song, chanting, music, food, or art-making,

you not only allow joy to be in service to the healing of your personal grief,

you begin to understand

the technology of JOY

in healing the entire planetary reality.

How do you "understand" this?

It is not intellectual understanding

It is embodied knowing.

You physically,

emotionally,

and energetically

FEEL it

And the only way we can feel,

Homecoming

as humans,

is through the body.

The code of Love reminds you

that choosing to be in your body

is the single most important thing you can do

to heal the planet.

What causes us to leave the body?

Trauma

and lower states of consciousness

such as fear, worry, doubt, shame, guilt, or anxiety

that are all by-products of that trauma.

What brings us back into our body?

BREATH

AND

PLEASURE.

Both states,

of either trauma response or

pleasure

impact our gene expression

and experience of dis-ease or health.

We shift epigenetic patterns across generations by choosing love over fear.

We shift out of dis-ease and into healing by choosing Love over fear.

We shift the choices we make in relationships by choosing Love over fear.

We shift the entire Earth grid and her climate structure by choosing Love over fear.

This choice, when chosen repeatedly, turns on higher frequencies within and around us,

so much that it shifts our reality and changes the course of history.

You cannot think LOVE

You FEEL Love.

And this feeling propels choices

And the choices provide deeper feeling

And this feedback loop creates new neural pathways in the brain

And this shapes our perception and sensation

And perception and sensation create our reality

And our reality is the summation of our choices.

The antidote to anything you don't want to be experiencing is

CHOICE.

If that choice is rooted in Love

Then not only do you begin to experience life as a more loving place to be

But you also begin to know on a deep cellular level

That you are

WORTHY

Of experiencing that kind of life.

And it is where

Choice and Self-worth are married

That

POSITIVE, LASTING

CHANGE

BECOMES

ABSOLUTE.

We will never come to this absolute

through some external source

We will only ever arrive where we want to be

by listening to that precious internal voice of Love.

Lastly, it needs to be stated that

JOY and PLEASURE have become perverted

so as to promote consumption.

When we reinstate JOY and PLEASURE

as SACRED,

as technologies for cellular and energetic healing,

we subvert an entire capitalistic model

rooted in FEAR.

This system is rooting for our scarcity.

By returning pleasure back to an expression of divinity,

we are rooting for ABUNDANCE.

And not just abundance for a select few,

but abundance for ALL of existence.

You have trained at an Olympic level to be rewarded for your Martyrdom.

Perhaps this training happened at an ancestral level,

a societal level,

or due to a specific event.

The problem with the School of Martyrdom, however,

is that you can never fully graduate

because there will

ALWAYS

be more to GIVE.

Accepting these Codes of Love

grants you admission to a new school.

In this new school you experience instantaneous reward,

success,

"graduation", if you will,

every time you choose Love over fear.

It's really that simple.

It's not easy.

Just like the Sacraments channeled within this book.

Homecoming

These 7 Sacraments of the Goddess are simple, but not easy... yet.

These codes and sacraments are only not easy because of the way our current society system is set up,

but the beautiful paradox, of course,

is that the more you practice and embody these tenets

the easier they become

and therefore THE SHIFT becomes

for the entire collective to birth the New Earth.

Congratulations on choosing to be alive

in a body

at this time.

You can,

and you will,

and you already are

making it through the labor pains and contractions.

Birth is imminent,

And so is the life you dream of living.

All that's required

is your choice to

choose it.

Thank you

Beloved reader, thank you for choosing to deeply invest in yourself. I am honored to be a part of your homecoming journey. If this book sparked something for you, and you'd like to go deeper, please join me for 1:1 mentorship, online courses, workshops and international retreats.

If you feel inspired to write a review of this book, please do so via Amazon, Goodreads, or elsewhere; heartfelt reviews are the greatest gift you can offer an author.

For more information about my offerings, and how to stay in touch, please visit www.sarah-grady.com or follow me on social media: @sarahbgrady. I look forward to our paths crossing. And no matter where it takes you, may your homecoming be blessed.

With Love,

Sarah

About the Author

Photo: Jacilyn Ledford

Sarah Grady is a former psychotherapist turned spiritual teacher, author and doula. She guides women who feel lost in their lives to find their way back home. Through her unique process of *Homecoming*, Sarah teaches women how to access the wisdom of their bodies so they can unapologetically align with a life that lights them up. Sarah has extensively trained in the realms of psychology, performing arts, energy healing and embodiment. For over a decade, she has woven together each modality into a unique body of work that supports women in birthing not just babies, but also themselves. She has personally used this work to move herself from a state of burnout to balance. She is on a mission to support every woman in claiming their birthright to this balance within themselves, their relationships and the Earth.

To find out more about Sarah and her work please visit www.sarah-grady.com

About the Publisher

R ed Thread Publishing is an all-female publishing company on a mission to support 10,000 women to become successful published authors and thought leaders. Through the transformative work of writing & telling our stories we are not only changed as individuals, but we are also changing the global narrative & thus the world.

www.redthreadbooks.com

CPSIA information can be obtained
at www.ICGtesting.com
Printed in the USA
LVHW082235310722
724842LV00030B/838

9 781955 683197